# VOTE FOR PANT

**Sorabh Pant** is a comedian and an author. His comedy specials—*My Baby Thinks I'm Funny* (2016) and *Make India Great Again* (2018)—were released on Amazon Prime Video.

He's the ex-founder of *East India Comedy*, a former news debate panellist and has hosted 200 YouTube Lives which have received almost eight billion views on Youtube.com/1phuntru. He releases free stand-up videos regularly on his YouTube channel, Pant On Fire.

His previous books include *The Wednesday Soul: The Afterlife with Sunglasses* and *Under Delhi*. Follow him on Twitter, Instagram, LinkedIn and his YouTube and Facebook channels.

Also by the author

*Pawan: The Flying Accountant*

# VOTE FOR PANT
**BUT, DON'T!**

## SORABH PANT

RUPA

Published by
Rupa Publications India Pvt. Ltd 2022
7/16, Ansari Road, Daryaganj
New Delhi 110002

*Sales centres:*
Allahabad Bengaluru Chennai
Hyderabad Jaipur Kathmandu
Kolkata Mumbai

Copyright © Sorabh Pant 2022

All rights reserved.

No part of this publication may be reproduced, transmitted,
or stored in a retrieval system, in any form or by any means,
electronic, mechanical, photocopying, recording or otherwise,
without the prior permission of the publisher.

The views and opinions expressed in this book are the author's own
and the facts are as reported by him which have been
verified to the extent possible, and the publishers are
not in any way liable for the same.

ISBN: 978-93-5520-219-2

First impression 2022

10 9 8 7 6 5 4 3 2 1

The moral right of the author has been asserted.

Printed at HT Media Ltd, Greater Noida

This book is sold subject to the condition that it shall not, by way of trade
or otherwise, be lent, resold, hired out, or otherwise circulated,
without the publisher's prior consent, in any form of binding
or cover other than that in which it is published.

# Contents

*Disclaimer* — *vii*
*Timelines* — *ix*

1. Your Future, Dear Beloved Leader — 1
2. Tax-Free Party: Agenda — 10
3. Did [Redacted] Take My Joke? — 21
4. Making Bribery Great Again — 28
5. Fraud: The Golden Ticket — 36
6. How to Use Motivational Speakers to End Unemployment — 49
7. Population: Not My Problem! — 58
8. Air India Sold! — 68
9. Income Tax: Note of Thanks — 80
10. Buying the News — 89
11. WhatsApp vs News: Lies — 98
12. (An Outdated Chapter) on Nepotism in Bollywood — 110
13. Cancel Woke Culture? — 129
14. China is World — 142
15. Pant Ki Baat: Episode One And Last — 167

*And Another Thing…* — 181
*Acknowledgments* — 185

# *Disclaimer*

Since some of you are prone to overreactions about a (any) PM, so it's best to clarify.

PM could stand for particulate matter, post meridiem, picometre, personal message, private message, pulse modulation, plasma membrane, post-mortem, particle mesh, phase modulation, Principia Mathematica, pretty man or Pant male.

You can assume that I aspire to be pollution, a unit of measurement, in your inbox, a biological term, a computer term, a book about math, death, myself or myself.

It may also imply Prime Minister.

But, you thought it—not me.

Because I have zero interest or chance of becoming that.

Additionally, any reference to any person, living or dead, mentioned in this book is purely coincidental. All of these people are from an alternate universe—also called India—but completely different in the sense that it is a world where people have a sense of humour and do not have extra time to file suits on behalf of people who were not offended in the first place.

The following are a mix of original thoughts, inspired by my old stand-ups (always get inspired by the best) and random thoughts I may have shared on social media platforms. It may also form the basis for future stand-up; the advantage here is that you don't have to hear it in my voice.

So, congratulations.

These are thoughts about India, her issues, problems—both real and imaginary—and will help confirm why I should be some kind of PM. But, not the PM.

Some chapters also have solutions to problems that can be implemented immediately. I serve you, the Indian people and I come here to save you from yourself.

PM also stands for (P)religious Messiah.

# *Timelines*

After I signed on to write this book, the words just flowed. Within two months, half the book was finished and I began thinking maybe I should write a book every month the next year and use that fortune to buy out Flipkart.

Then my publishers told me that the release date was pushed because of the pandemic. Apparently, my publishers had not even bothered to find a vaccine, which is highly unprofessional. How can publishers not do basic things like hustle up production of a biological tool that provides active acquired immunity to a particular infectious disease? I should have published with Poonawalla Press or Oxford (Zeneca) Publishers or waited for an offer from Covaxine Self-Publishing.

Either way, a pandemic is a watertight reason for delay and only a few would argue against it. But, given that this book was about trending topics, and the pandemic was trending more than anything, it made little sense to finish this book by 2020. So like any professional procrastinator, I completely stopped working on this book because I am an idiot. Big mistake! I forgot about it and moved on to other scams to make money.

In January 2021, my publishers resurfaced—kudos to them, given that this pandemic thing was still around—and we got into talks about releasing the book tentatively by June 2021. 'Will you be able to finish the book by 1 April 2021?' they asked.

I said, 'Of course, the first half took barely a month. I'll nail this by then for sure.' I did not. More delays were caused this time because of my lack of professionalism.

By the time the release was scheduled, it struck me that my publishers might demand for their advance money. So, mainly to ensure I don't lose that money, I decided to resume work on the pending manuscript.

It also helped that for 20 days, I had the house to myself because my wife and kids had gone to her mother's house. I could have had multiple affairs and hosted a couple of Bollywood drug parties (which most Indians think happen so often)—but instead I decided to write.

I think.

As I write this before I have finished the manuscript, I hope if you are reading this, it probably has been completed. I tell you all this because a lot of content is topical and a lot of those topics may have changed: Mallya may have been extradited to India and become a parliamentarian to stay innocent, nepotism may have once again become the norm for Bollywood, petrol prices may have crossed ₹500 per drop, the Indian cricket team may have been replaced by AI robots, doctors in India may be armed by those robots to fight people trying to beat them up and printing press across the country may have all gathered junk and collapsed.

Whatever the circumstances, this book dealing with current affairs was written across a span of one-and-a-half year. So, excuse the tone, content and the updates of the world as mentioned in the book. If my foolish 'insights' into a topic age badly because of a change in circumstances or the movement of time, blame my publishers for not creating a third vaccine instead of wasting their time asking me to write this book.

It also must be noted that I am not a journalist. I'm mostly an idiot who has access to some information—most of it I think is correct, some may not be. My only source of information is Google and then news portals, coupled with some words and conjectures of other people.

So, please do not treat this as a journalistic endeavor—this is just some dude with an outdated laptop (that I currently can't afford to update) typing about musings which only 12 people might read.

# 1

## *Your Future, Dear Beloved Leader*

### Introduction

I was born in 1981, the same year when Infosys was started in Pune by N.R. Narayana Murthy. Many people have called me the Infosys of Indian comedy. In fact, I've gotten exhausted with the comparison. One journalist described it as follows:

> 'Sorabh Pant is commonly known as "the Infosys of Indian comedy" because of the sheer impact on the country and revenue he's generated. In 2020, Infosys generated $12.78 billion; Sorabh's revenue is considered by experts to be almost twice that in February 2020 alone. Narayana Murthy has reportedly told employees to aspire to be more like Mr Pant and an HR policy instituted on 8 December 2013 stated: "In celebration of this day when the esteemed comedian Sorabh Pant finished five years in comedy, we would urge all employees to kindly get haircuts like Sorabh to get an aerodynamic feel that

> would inspire them to reach his heights." Unfortunately, Infosys—as incredible an organization as it is—can never touch the high standards Mr Pant has set with his stand-up videos titled 'Your Friends Are Haraamis', 'Game of Thrones Nudity Explained' and 'Goa and Penguins' and of course 'Celebrity Kids That Should Not Have Kids…'

This was published in the *The Times of India*, page no. 86. Since TOI usually publishes around 60 pages, many readers of TOI might not have received the remaining 26 pages and hence are unaware of this important piece of news. The journalist, Mousami Joshi, also disappeared and was reported missing; TOI denies that such a journalist ever existed, which is surely part of a larger cover-up operation.

The year 1981 was also the year when Yuvraj Singh, M.S. Dhoni and Roger Federer were born. While the three of them won World Cups, grand slams, IPLs etc., their stand-up never got almost three lakh views. Sorry to say, but that is another win for Pant (me).

Truth aside, let me give you a quick introduction in case you're reading this book out of the blue and have no clue who I am.

My name is Sorabh Pant. I'm a stand-up comedian and an author. This is my fourth book, but first non-fiction title. My first three novels, *The Wednesday Soul: The Afterlife with Sunglasses*, *Under Delhi* and *Pawan: The Flying Accountant* would all be commissioned by OTT platforms by the time you would be reading this. One of them has been commissioned for over ₹8 crore—sorry, Amish Tripathi. I'm hoping you are reading this in 2028 when the possibility of this being actually true may be higher—though, not by much.

You may recognize me from there.

In 2014, I co-founded a comedy collective called *East India Comedy* (EIC). We thought we could dominate the Indian comedy scene like the East India Company, but with zero deaths, slavery, inhumanity and blatant robbery. Frankly, we could have named it something else; we were unaware of history, baggage and other things that allow people to have a brain. EIC did well and we achieved a reasonable amount of success with shows like *The Ghantas* (an annual award show on the worst of Bollywood), *EIC Outrage* (a weekly news/issue-based show) and brand deals with alcohol companies that ensured the above two didn't leave us broke.

Over the course of three years, we made some money, expanded the team and got some 300 million views online and spent a lot of time thinking how much success we could have had had we called ourselves *East India Bakchod*. My fellow comedians in EIC—Kunal Rao, Sapan Verma, Sahil Shah, Atul Khatri, Azeem Banatwalla and Angad Singh Ranyal—remain my closest friends in the industry, even though some define them as 'leftist liberals that are anti-national vermins who should all lose citizenship of India'.

You may recognize me from there.

In 2017, I left *East India Comedy* in pursuit of making more money because my wife caused two kids to appear magically (I only have a vague idea how) and god knows we needed the money, which I succeeded in making till March 2020. We'll come back to that...

I also toured a live stand-up comedy show in 14 countries called *Rant of the Pant*—where I ranted about important issues that I didn't understand, preceded by my Amazon Prime Special, *My Baby Thinks I'm Funny*, where I used my son's birth for profit and jokes, and my 2018 Amazon Prime Special, *Make India Great Again*, where I tried to make political jokes that wouldn't get me killed and ones which turned into political jokes that were not as sharp as I wanted them to be.

You may recognize me from there.

You may have also seen me on my appearances in news debates—which I stopped doing as frequently in 2019 because I released a stand-up clip making fun of news debates and coincidentally, they stopped calling me.

You won't recognize me from there.

For a considerably long time—till about 2019—I used to make a lot of political jokes. That's when I realized I have kids and a family and despite what people will tell you about freedom of speech in India, it's not as free as the dumb may think. Despite constantly attempting to be neutral in my jokes, I was not neutral enough for some people. Because for these people unless you LOVE and ADORE and WORSHIP their dear leader (whichever leader it happens to be at that time), you are funded by a foreign government or a rival political party and should promptly move to Kazakhstan. Who will pay for your tickets to these countries is a question they are not willing to answer.

I've been accused of being a fan of the other party by every other party. The BJP fans called me a Congress agent, Congress fans called me a BJP agent and the AAP fans called me for donations. Currently, I have received no donations from any of these parties, which is really disappointing. By their own logic, I should be on the payroll of every political party in India.

Not for the first time though, making political jokes comes with wonderful psychos sending you death threats. I had received the same in 2014, 2015, 2016, 2017 and 2018 with clockwork regularity—like renewing an annual contract with murderers. I took them on the chin because I've never been a fan of life in the first place; I mean I love living, it's great, but I'm not too afraid of the alternative.

And then came 2019.

In December 2019, I received 19 death threats for a 'political' joke I had made in 2017. It shows how long it takes for some people to understand—or in this case completely misunderstand—a joke. Two years is the time period it took their brains to comprehend what I was (not) trying to say. The threats detailed how I would be killed as well as various creative methods that would be applied. One man said, *'Saale tera sarr kaat ke football khelega mein* [I will cut off your head and play football with it].'

It's nice of this man to promote sports in India, especially football. I imagine Sunil Chhetri (a man I deeply admire) would have mixed feelings about such a threat: on one end it is a psychopath threatening to kill another human being, but on the other hand, it might be a good advertisement for Indian Super League. Imagine it: man threatens me that he'll chop off my head and play football with it. He does. My head rolls down, he paints it black and white, kicks it, a whistle goes off and 22 players kick my dead head around for 90 minutes, interspersed with advertising for products related to heads: shampoos, rackets, etc.

It could lead to what I didn't really get much of in life: viewership.

Also, my head is quite nicely shaped to be a football and the lack of hair ensures there's a consistent surface area—barring my nose and lips, which I'm assuming are pretty disposable once my head is chopped off.

Obviously, I was not this relaxed at the time I received those death threats. A lot of the threats came from men holding swords and guns (which may indicate what the joke was about)—not joking—as if their Facebook display picture was showing me the suspect's face and mode of attack, kind of like *Street Fighter* or *Tekken*. (Yes, I'm old and refuse to update these references to *Dragon Ball FighterZ* or *Virtua Fighter*).

The worst part about the whole thing was the date: 31 December 2019, i.e., New Year's Eve. My only resolution that year was to not die. It's not an ideal way to bring in the new year—10, 9, 8, 7, 6, 5, 4, 3, 2, 1...MURDER!—but it sort of typified 2019 for me.

The year had been a bit of a challenge, to say the least, on a professional (as talked about above), personal (will discuss in a future book/stand-up show), emotional, financial, global and the local front. Everything was aligned to push me up against a wall. And through the year, I looked at 2020 with hope. Mathematically, aesthetically, it's such a wonderful figure. It exemplifies perfect vision, a perfect score in archery (I think) and my second favourite format of cricket. It's also a leap year and a leap year implies joy by its definition. Frogs leap, you leap for joy, a leap of hope—it implies flight and jumping, all joyful things.

I decided to get fitter (I did), lose weight (I did), get more focused (I did), more relaxed (I did) and expected 2020 to be the best year of my life. And I know many people who felt that way—the year itself inspired this thought.

By the time the year actually caught on, most of humanity was wishing we had the option to leap over the entire year.

While protests rang out across India and many parts

of the world for different reasons, trade wars escalated and de-escalated, Russia and Saudi Arabia fought over oil prices and fire raged in Australia, we felt the chaos across the world, but somehow most of us could deal with it.

Then somebody decided they wanted to eat a bat soup, mildly flavored with pangolin faeces...

And everything changed, arguably, forever.

Both these things—the threats and the pandemic—combined to help me realize one essential truth: I have two kids, one wife and a hefty EMI to pay. I have to remain alive and I have to pay off my loan.

That's the reason I'm writing this book—to help me pay a small portion of my monthly EMI. Given books barely make money, this will help pay about 72 per cent of one month's EMI. If you're bored and want to do some math, this can help you figure out how much I got paid for this book and how much my EMI is and, in consequence, my net worth.

I would also like to convince you through this book that I should be PM (one of the PMs mentioned earlier) and enumerate the reasons why. Because let's be honest, there's nothing more profitable than politics. You either make money illegally or you earn power legally and both are abundantly rich currencies.

Additionally, if you are PM and someone sends you a death threat, then that person can be tried for sedition. And that would be a massive upgrade from having to report threats on Instagram or Facebook or YouTube and occasionally getting no response.

So, please vote for me in the next election. I promise to be the best Particulate Matter this nation has never seen.

## small thoughts

*News debates seem to be losing a bit of steam in the public discourse which usually means they're going to get more desperate to make them relevant, which means we all better watch out.*

*With that in mind, I propose some rules for news debates in India. These could also be the rules for advertisers; even though they rarely let ethics overrule reach, they advertise on my YouTube as well.*

*Either way, here are some simple rules that should be followed: Every person in a debate gets to talk and the sentence has to be more than, 'Let me speak, please.' If they're not, then the anchor has to pay for 100 minutes of free international talk time for the panellists.*

- *If the anchor talks for more than 50 per cent of the debate, they have to forego 51 per cent of their salary for 50 per cent of the year.*
- *If the number of panellists in a debate is more than the members of a cricket team, that debate shall hereby have to be called a cacophony or a chaos or a mela and not a debate.*
- *If the words 'anti-national', 'Pakistan', 'China' are mentioned on a debate not involving the above three topics, then each panellist gets a round trip to Beijing (paid window seat as a throw-in).*
- *The anchor should be free to mute any panellist they deem worthy because while a lot of abuse gets thrown toward the anchors, a lot of panellists on news debates are rough.*
- *If an anchor shares more than three bits of false news in a*

*week, then the panellists can spread four bits of false news about the anchor without any legal repercussions.*
- *Viewers have the discretion to not watch debates.*

*Okay bye.*

# 2

## *Tax-Free Party: Agenda*

Before I explain to you my thoughts and opinions on every issue under the sun—specifically those I don't understand—I need a platform. Every politician needs a political party, mainly to ensure that they don't have to pay for the deposit for standing for an election directly. Why have personal expenses when they can be billed to the company? Now it's up to you to decide how serious I am about this (not at all serious) and whether this is all satire.

It's exhausting that in India one has to mention that one is being satirical while doing satire because there's such a large portion of this country that takes everything seriously. So here I am telling you that this is a purely satirical exercise—I would politely like to tell you to send your outrage in another direction. Use the metaphorical Narmada Dam of your mind and divert your liquid thoughts towards probably protesting about the Narmada Dam, or whatever it is that you care about.

Here goes my pitch for my new (and not real) political party…

On 8 November 2016, Narendra Modi—voted world's no. 1 leader by UNESCO (courtesy WhatsApp rumours)—said the most famous line by an Indian Prime Minister since Nehru, 'At the stroke of the midnight hour…' And yes, I decided to put Nehru and Modi in the same sentence because it will annoy political zealots on both sides.

PM Modi said, 'We have decided that the ₹500 and ₹1,000 currency notes presently in use will no longer be legal tender.'[1]

Despite a few deaths (big deal—we have so much population, right?) and a general downturn in the economy (I base this on the economy of my own bank account, my friend's bank accounts and anecdotal evidence from social media and perhaps reality) for a few months and marginal changes in income tax collections and with some 'experts' saying (on social media and so may be questionable) that the cost of printing the money was more than the money earned by demonetization, a lot of us thought it was a good idea—in concept.

And even if we didn't, we were told that if we don't find it good, we were corrupt Panama Paper-named sedition-hungry anti-nationals. Realistically, a move to demonetize India was a great idea to clean out black money from the system. Even though it led to the ₹2,000 note being launched, which became the bane of every Indian's wallet for years, just roaming around looking for change for that annoying note could take weeks, months, sometimes a year and lead us to wait for another demonetization so that the dratted note would not be valid any more.

But, it was good. It's for our own good. Because… because…it'll reduce the amount of black money in the economy. Right? Right? Of course. Yes. Right?

---

[1] 'Withdrawal of Legal Tender Status for ₹500 and ₹1000 Notes: RBI Notice', *Reserve Bank of India*, 8 November 2016, https://rbi.org.in/Scripts/BS_PressReleaseDisplay.aspx?prid=38520. Accessed on 15 February 2022.

Then soon after this, the late Arun Jaitley—voted no. 1 finance minister by chartered accountants (courtesy WhatsApp rumours)—said, 'We are at the process of making history, with the launch of goods and services tax.'[2]

Initially, GST was more confusing to understand than the Jacqueline Fernandez hit, *Mrs Serial Killer* back when I wrote it. But, over time we adjusted to it. And paid the extra three per cent to five per cent tax that we were supposed to—because why not?[3] We are patriots and we must express ourselves as one with our wallets and streamlining.

GST reduced leakages in the system, even if the government made you pay it before you got the money—that is another story. And state governments did not receive their share of GST for months, but, that's their problem, right? Not ours.

GST was actually much-needed despite teething troubles. We were all like, 'Great move. Because centralization and transparency and reduction of corruption. Everything is above board.'

Then Narendra Modi—voted BFF of the Year by Amit Shah (courtesy rumours on private WhatsApp chats)—said, 'In today's day, an ordinary Aadhar Card has become the symbol of people's empowerment.'[4]

Yes, Aadhar Card has become the symbol of my empowerment and my old Pan Card became roach paper.

---

[2] 'We Are In The Process Of Making History, Says Jaitley At GST Launch Event', NDTV, 30 June 2017, https://www.ndtv.com/video/news/news/we-are-in-the-process-of-making-history-says-jaitley-at-gst-launch-event-461663. Accessed on 2 March 2022.

[3] 'All your queries on GST answered', *The Hindu*, 29 March 2017, https://www.thehindu.com/news/resources/all-your-queries-on-gst-answered/article14585151.ece1. Accessed on 16 February 2022.

[4] https://www.youtube.com/watch?v=leI8RVd-s_4. Accessed on 2 March 2022.

Every government that comes into power insists on changing the mode of ID in this country—whether it's the ration card to Pan Card to Aadhar Card to People's Card (2024) to UID Card (2029) to Birthday Card (2034).

But look, Aadhar Card was only a minor inconvenience. Let's say it's all good. It's centralized identity. We should all, as citizens, be more transparent, open, declare our funds, help the country, not indulge in black money, not be devious about our source of funds—a good citizen of the nation.

Right? Right? Of course, right?

According to polls right group, Association for Democratic reforms, 70 per cent of poll funding for political parties in India is from unknown sources.[5] If you were afraid of those dragons in *Game of Thrones*, be alarmed, this is more frightening.

According to them, this is the case for well-known parties:[6]

Samajwadi Party—94 per cent of poll funding source unknown

Congress—83 per cent unknown

BJP—65 per cent unknown

Akali Dal—86 per cent unknown

If that's true, that's incredible. Imagine you filed your income tax returns and 94 per cent of your income was unknown. What do you think would happen? Do you think you would win Amazon vouchers from the income tax

---

[5] PTI, 'National parties collected Rs 3,370 cr from unknown sources in 2019-20: ADR', *Business Standard*, 31 August 2021, https://www.business-standard.com/article/current-affairs/national-parties-collected-rs-3-370-cr-from-unknown-sources-in-2019-20-adr-121083100852_1.html. Accessed on 9 February 2022.

[6] '68% Income Of Political Parties Is From Unknown Sources, Reveals New Study', *Association for Democratic Reforms*, 30 January 2017, https://www.adrindia.org/content/68-income-political-parties-unknown-sources-reveals-new-study. Accessed on 15 February 2022.

department? Or do you think there would be legal action and possibly jail time for you?

Ninety-four per cent.

Ninety-four!

With that high a percentage, you could've gotten into Delhi University, even on the nineteenth merit list. It gets considerably worse. Political parties also enjoy tax exemptions. Because why pay taxes on undeclared income anyway?

I'm not a CA or a lawyer, so I may get some of this wrong. If so, do correct me and let me know if I'm wrong on social media. But, as per my understanding, here's how this goes.

As per the Section 13A of the IT Act, political parties don't have to pay taxes on income from house property or voluntary contributions, or capital gains, or conveniently on income from other sources.[7] Why not include the whole universe? 'Other sources' is such a wonderfully vague term, it could apply to literally anything.

A political party in India could sell the moon for a voluntary donation and the entire lunar body would be tax exempt as 'income from other sources'.

But, it's not all easy for them—they have to pay taxes on head salaries and income from business or profession. What a tough life. That must amount to a few lakhs per decade.

If you ask for or read comments by the authorities or those concerned over why such an exemption was required in the first place, they say things like, 'It was to promote political participation.'

---

[7]'Special provision relating to incomes of political parties', *Income Tax Department*, https://www.incometaxindia.gov.in/_layouts/15/dit/pages/viewer. aspx?grp=act&cname=cmsid&cval=102120000000058034&searchfilter=. Accessed on 15 February 2022.

Really?

Do we need MORE politics in India? Has any Indian ever woken up and thought, 'You know food and shelter and employment and all is okay, but what would really make me happier is to know that we have MORE politicians in India. That sounds delicious and would feed my family.'

Till February 2019, 2,143 political parties registered with the Election Commission.[8] Let that sink in—two. thousand. one. hundred. forty. three. political. parties. Does the chairperson of the Central Board of Direct Taxes genuinely think that we need to 'promote' political participation in India? Are 2,143 parties not enough promotion?

If anything, they should charge them more tax so that there could be less political parties in India. Can you imagine if 1,500 start-ups across India were to be effectively tax-exempt? Meerut (I've never been there but am sure it's great) would become Silicon Valley. Every city in India would be a bastion of innovation and invention. We would be atmanirbhar (self-reliant) in precisely one week.

Instead, what we effectively get is a brand new political party every month, figuring new ways to manipulate the system.

And by the way, this is not even the end of how bad things are. Some of you may already know this, but most of you may not, so, read on...

Credit to be given where it's due. The BJP has been TRYING to make politics transparent. Except, they're constantly

---

[8]PTI, 'India now has 2,293 political parties, 149 registered between February & March', *The Economic Times*, 17 March 2019, https://economictimes.indiatimes.com/news/elections/lok-sabha/india/india-now-has-2293-political-parties-149-registered-between-february-march/articleshow/68451605.cms?from=mdr. Accessed on 15 February 2022.

giving mixed signals. First, Arun Jaitley said, 'In accordance with the suggestion made by the Election Commission, the maximum amount of cash donation that a political party can receive will be ₹2,000, from any one person.'[9]

That's great. It means that no organization—charitable, profitable, whatever—can legally 'bribe' their way to curry favours. Except, it's not. Because then they went on to introduce a wonderful concept called electoral bonds. Here's apparently how this concept works: an institution of electoral trust was created. Again, I'm not a very intelligent or smart or even vaguely intelligible person, but this is what I think this means. Let's say I am a company (Pant's Pants Garments Inc.) I create a trust (PPG Trust). I give money to the trust. Apparently, as per the rule on electoral bonds—NOBODY can know how or what or to whom the trust gave that money. Instead of my company, my trust gave the money to a political party, through the electoral trust. And the electoral trust, which will ensure clean money, will forward it to the party.

If you didn't understand what the hell I'm talking about, let me explain it to you in simpler English. Here's how an electoral bond works (I think):

You give money to a bank.

They give you an electoral bond.

You take that electoral bond and give it anonymously to a political party.

And the party doesn't know who gave it, neither do we,

---

[9] Dey, Abhishek. 'Will the Rs 2,000 cap on cash donations for political parties bring more transparency in the system?', *Scroll.in,* 1 February 2017, https://scroll.in/article/828281/will-the-rs-2000-cap-on-cash-donations-for-political-parties-bring-more-transparency-in-the-system. Accessed on 9 February 2022.

neither do the people that take care of taxation and monetary transactions, etc.

It's like surprise Santa.

'Who gave me this ₹2 crore?'

'Nobody knows. Happy Diwali to you!'

And all this is done anonymously. So we will have no idea who gave money to whom. Eighty-nine per cent of all known donations to parties come from corporates.[10]

With electoral bonds, it 'could' now mean that there would be 89 per cent of donations with unknown origin stories. Indian politics is like the IPL. There are so many sponsors, we just can't confirm their names.

After electoral bonds, corporates can own politics and we'll never know. There's zero accountability, as said by Ravish Kumar (Yes, I named him. I will also name Arnab in two lines. So, you can stay calm.)

Ravish Kumar said, 'Now the companies won't need to show in their books who they donated the money to. You give so much money to someone and you won't have to tell anyone about it.'[11]

He's absolutely right. Right now, as a civilian, you need an Aadhar Card to buy a hole inside a medu vada. But political parties can fart golden doughnuts, that too with no paperwork.

Arnab.

(There I named him. Happy?)

---

[10]Deka, Kaushik. 'Political funding: Who pays for the party?', India Today, 9 November 2018, https://www.indiatoday.in/magazine/the-big-story/story/20181119-political-funding-who-pays-for-the-party-1384158-2018-11-09. Accessed on 15 February 2022.

[11]'Do Electoral Bonds Legitimise Anonymous Funding of Political Parties?', *NDTV YouTube*, 27 November 2019, https://www.youtube.com/watch?v=S3BkFrCzZuQ. Accessed on 15 February 2022.

The guys who made the Aadhar Card mandatory don't need it. That's amazing. In summary, this may be corporatizing corruption in the epicentre of black money in India. This is politics. And all of them seem to be in cahoots for this plan.

Usually, whenever the central government initiates any legislation, other parties object. In this case, the response from the top tier of political leaders in India was quieter than the crowd at a football match after COVID-19. All political parties pretend they are moralistic and above each other, but in this case they are not. All of them—INC, AAP, TMC, etc., remained eerily quiet.

Their words are much like the amount of tax they pay, which is 0 per cent (roughly). Just to contextualize this for you even more:

Between 2004–05 and 2014–15, the amount of unaccounted funds political parties received was ₹7,833 crore.[12] This is what that amount could buy us (courtesy my probably erroneous calculations):

- Four-and-a-half Worli Sea Link
- Two metros in Mumbai
- 28 Bahubali sequels
- 87 per cent of Vijay Mallya
- 2.6 Statues of Unity

It's pretty clear what unites all political parties in India. No further comments.

---

[12]PTI, 'Political parties got Rs 7,833 crore from unknown sources in last 11 years: Report', *The Economic Times*, 24 January 2017, https://economictimes.indiatimes.com/news/politics-and-nation/political-parties-got-rs-7833-crore-from-unknown-sources-in-last-11-years-report/articleshow/56762772.cms?from=mdr. Accessed on 9 February 2022.

## What Would I Do Before I Become PM

That I will soon become Private Message of India is inevitable, obviously. But, here's my solution to you, the Indian people. Why should we be accountable to political parties when they are not accountable to us? So I would hereby like to launch my brand new political party.

It's called the Tax-Free Party. I have no responsibility towards the country. Everything I do is tax free. You buy tickets for my shows? No GST on that. It's a donation, it's anonymous. You are my electoral trust.

I need 100 members to start a political party—if you're interested in having zero fiscal responsibility while being hypocritical enough to call people that don't pay taxes 'criminals' and pretending you give a toss about the nation, then join me.

Since I have no money, you log on to taxfreeparty.com and register the domain and then send me the password because if I learned anything from wanting power, it's about knowing when to delegate.

For legal reasons, I must mention this again that this is a satirical piece. I do not plan to start any political party, neither now, nor in future. In any case, whichever Indian political party you're deluded enough to unyieldingly support, please know that all of them should be called the Tax-Free Party.

Some of them pretend otherwise, but most of their dedication to the people rarely extends beyond their own self-interests. There's 0 per cent source of this information.

## small thoughts

I live in Mumbai, the financial capital of India. But, one of our biggest problem seems to be that only five roads (that are actually roads) seem to be existing in this financial capital. The remaining have potholes or speed breakers the size of my dad's paunch (or my paunch) or an uneven layout that ensures that your car is dented from below (a rare achievement).

There was a narrow lane outside my house that went under construction six times in the three years I was there. At one point, the workers had dug half the road and piled the mud and insides of the road on the other half. This led to an adventurous ride for commuters for whom this was the shortest route to get to Bandra Station. They had a mountain and a valley in the middle of the city, but the ungrateful wretches complained. Shameful.

At one point at dusk, I saw one of the workers standing atop a cement mound and urinating right at its peak. He had the joy and confidence of someone that had in fact achieved this feat from the top of the Everest. And this is an inspiring tale. There should be a rule in India: if the lane outside your house has to be repaired once every six months, then you should have the right to go urinate at the office of whoever is in charge of that road. You don't have to actually do it, but have the option to do so.

This is not a real solution. Please do find a urinal.

# 3

# Did [Redacted] Take My Joke?

Every politician needs script writers. Some of them are IIM, IIT graduates and they get hefty salaries to ensure that the right thing is said. I save the Indian people this fee because I write for myself, as I have been doing since 2008. Additionally, I will prove to you that the jokes and words I write are already pre-approved by politicians with the following story.

In 2019, I thought I was going to get famous. I had released a stand-up clip prior to the General Elections and it was spreading furiously on WhatsApp. I know it makes my level of success seem really sad that going 'viral' on WhatsApp is my idea of fame, but don't judge me because I'm a sad, little man.

I try to attempt neutrality in my stand-up about politics because being dismissive and condescending about people's beliefs seems undemocratic and apathetic. Some people curse me for being a centrist or being neutral, but, as the Internet has taught me, people will curse you irrespective of what you say or don't. I don't believe that your political opinions necessarily imply you're a terrible person, but occasionally your motivations behind having such opinions does.

The intention of a lot of my stand-up was to call out the

bullshit of everyone and especially the party in power. People who shit on comedians for making jokes on the current government seem unaware that we've been making jokes on standing governments since 2008. The only difference then was that the number of people telling us to go to Uzbekistan was one—the tourism minister of Uzbekistan.

Politics has now become a religion (ironic) and educated people have started treating politicians like demigods. Now, it is said, 'Oh, I worship the God of Divisiveness, don't say anything about him or he will smite you with citizenship of another land', unlike before when it was said, 'Oh, I worship the God of Scams, don't say anything about him or he will smite you with increased taxes and more delayed flyovers.' It's honestly whichever 'religion' you find less evil.

Anyway, I had released a short video making quick and easy jokes on the BJP, AAP and Congress, but the video faded away and I thought that my unclaimed fame is over.

However, nothing is over until the IT Cell (and they exist for every party) say so. What one of the parties' IT Cell apparently did was that they took that video and edited out the jokes solely targeting their opposing party and re-released the video from their end. Now the opposing party's IT Cell could have done the same thing (edited the video with *their* opposing party's jokes and released it), but they were still unfamiliar with the Internet. They were still running around with a wire wondering how to shove it into their phones, 'Mummy, how to get Internet? Should I put DSN cable into landline?'

I'm not naming the parties in question, but I'm sure you can guess.

P.S.: A few months later, the other party did precisely the same with another video I had released a year back. I can't remember which bit it was, but it was a song about the BJP and Congress from which the said party removed jokes against their leader and released it—I was half glad for them that they were at least learning how to play the game, whatever 'game' it was.

Anyway, that new video of my edited stand-up went genuinely viral across a party's IT Cell. This time, I expected and awaited fame, but there was a slight issue: I had not watermarked my name on the video, so no one knew it was me. I'm amazing at marketing.

Here was the joke for your reference (I'm not sure I agree with it anymore):

'I'm not a fan of coalition governments because I think they legitimize inefficiency. If a coalition government is selected in India 2019 elections—*Ek PM se kaam nahi banega. Sabko mauka de do* [One PM won't do. Give everyone a chance]. Have six prime ministers.'

'Monday, Mayawati; Tuesday, Mamata Banerjee; Wednesday, one of the Reddys, take your pick; Thursday, whichever Thackeray agrees; Friday, a Yadav on Saturday; Sunday, Rahul Gandhi because government doesn't work on weekends.'

Now, before you figure out the loopholes in this joke, I'll point them out to you myself:

1. The government does work on weekends. (Depends on the government and also depends on whether there's a riot happening.)
2. The list of politicians for the week is not part of the same coalition. (Yes, if you're naive enough to believe

that coalitions are not based on agenda but one fixed ideology.)
3. This assumes that even with a coalition, Congress would only be able to cobble up a government. (Fair point, barely four Indian states would disagree.)
4. Even to take your scenario in consideration, Rahul would be PM for two out of seven days—that would be an unfair break-up for the coalition. (This is a coalition which imagines that Congress won 77 out of 270 seats getting 2/7votes. #Solved)

Anyway, this video went viral on pro-government WhatsApp groups—which means it showed up on my family WhatsApp groups. Random people started sending me messages like, 'Is this you? But, it can't be you—because the joke is funny.' I forwarded them the jokes about the BJP and they responded by saying, 'Those are not funny', which proves that for most people, comedy comes with agenda.

What happened next was interesting. [Redacted] apparently performed his version of my joke. And unlike me, everyone knows who he is, because you have to for various reasons. He relayed my joke at two to three rallies in his own mass speaker fashion, really hard-selling the joke. Now, I started getting messages from random people again telling me, 'Hey man. Why did you steal [Redacted]'s joke?'

Yes, really.

This was a conversation I had with someone:

'Why did you copy [Redacted]'s joke, man?'

'Er...it was my joke. I've been performing it since 2018. In fact, I had written that joke in my book in 2017!'

'So you stole your joke from a book?'

'It was my book!'

'You shouldn't steal jokes—you're a comedian.'

'Dude, [Redacted] took my joke.'

'Yeah, right. If you really think that, why don't you file a case against him?'

And thus ends the conversation because I won't and I don't want to do so for obvious reasons.

Honestly, what worried me even more was what a comedian friend of mine pointed out, 'Listen, man. Shouldn't you be worried that [Redacted] and you have the same sense of humour?' I thought about this for days—should I rethink my core values? And then I realized that it's not that we have the same sense of humour, it is that in this one case, we enjoyed the same punchline. And I enjoy punchlines, damn the agenda.

And maybe that's a good thing.

Of course, things got even more absurd. Because [Redacted 2] (ex-CM of a state) started doing [Redacted]'s version of my joke in rallies, the difference being he did so in Marathi. My joke had gone through Google translate and I was not even consulted.

I'm obviously not in favour of anyone stealing or copying my jokes. In this case maybe, they did so only as a rite of passage—this may be an endorsement of my joke writing abilities. Because comedians have had jokes stolen before: Kunal Kamra had his joke stolen by Raju Srivastava; Abijit Ganguly had a joke stolen by the Kapil Sharma Show; I had my joke taken by two mainstream politicians, so surely, I win. I'm not sure what I win but, there it goes.

I'd further like to reiterate that maybe the esteemed and respected Mr [Redacted] did not actually steal my joke. Maybe it was all coincidence. Maybe we both just stumbled upon the exact same thought at the exact same time, worded exactly the same way. I'm sure that's what happened. Yes, yes.

I'd just urge political parties to pay me if they decide, in future, to steal my jokes (unlike this case, where they obviously did not). I know they have the money, they may as well start sharing it with us.

Honestly, what worried me more about this whole incident was that both [Redacted] and [Redacted 2] executed and delivered the joke way better than me. That's my big cause of concern as a performer.

## What Will I Do When I Become PM

I will steal the speeches by all the current and previous politicians and mix and mash them together and create my own 'original' content. I will not stop there. People will eventually catch on that I'm doing such a thing and I will catch myself out before they can. My speeches will also copy the introductions by people and probably even their names.

I will be so shameless in my theft that it will be impossible to catch me because I've already caught myself.

Here are a few excerpts from my would-be speeches:

'People of India—no more exorbitant excise tax on liquor—I have a dream that one day this nation will rise up, live out the true meaning of its creed. It's me, Martin Luther King.'

'My defense programme? An eye for an eye will make the world blind. It's me, Gandhiji.'

'I will try and legalize medicinal marijuana. It is an ideal for which I am prepared to die. It's definitely not me, Nelson Mandela.'

## small thoughts

*Censorship is an interesting thing in India because as Indians we love telling people what they can and cannot watch; everyone's morals should be aligned to everyone else's till a point where saying nothing is the only thing that would face no censorship.*

*However, if you said nothing, that would offend the sound recordists and audio operators of India and you don't want to mess with them because they can make you sound like an idiot—so, the cycle is endless.*

*Since we want to censor everything in India on religious, moral, sexual, political, communal, community-based grounds, I propose a simple solution.*

*Various creators in India from YouTubers, filmmakers to singers, to comedians—totalling up to one million—need to anonymously come together and spend $10 each to pay the creators of South Park, Trey Parker and Matt Stone, and $10 million to create a season of South Park: Indian edition. Make it as offensive and as humanly as possible, produce it in the US, air it straight on a separate website, so no CEO of an OTT is responsible for it and sit back and watch the fun.*

*Trey and Matt don't care and have not cared for 25 years and then your joke about Mirzapur will sound so tame in comparison— no one will file a case leading you to trend on social media.*

*#BanSouthParkIndia*

# 4

# *Making Bribery Great Again*

One of the big downsides to the current Modi government has been a fall in India's ranking in the global corruption index—something that was a source of great pride for India. It is a matter of great worry that this noble Indian institute is losing relevance.

If you've been following the Corruption Perceptions Index—and honestly, who hasn't?—Corruption Perceptions Index is next to only *Game of Thrones* and the Football World Cup in capturing the world's attention. People cannot get enough of watching the Corruption Perceptions Index, which is currently in its twenty-first season. What twists and turns will happen in Season 26?

Will Denmark and New Zealand continue their gripping fight for being ranked no. 1 or no. 2 every year? That rivalry makes Djokovic versus Nadal pale in comparison. And sports analysts across the globe are watching with riveted interest. Will Somalia maintain its consistency as the most corrupt nation in the world? Or will South Sudan make a come from behind, grab to pip them from the position?

Will South Sudan make the ultimate statement and try and bribe the judges of the Corruption Perceptions Index to make it to the no. 1 spot? And more importantly, for

Indian and Pakistani newspapers: will India continue losing to Pakistan in the rankings? Is corruption the reverse of the Cricket World Cup? That is truly something worth pondering.

And if you think I'm being ironic, every single time these rankings come on, every newspaper and news channel—on both sides of the border—makes comparisons. We continue competing even on this front.

Are we losing sight of what is important?

An example: I went to get my passport made. Having travelled globally for work, my passports tend to be renewed every four years, which may qualify me for the post of the PM. I showed up at the passport office. And I was surprised to find that the entire process took just one hour—from entry to exit. This is quicker than getting a visa on arrival at Bangkok airport—it was shocking.

I had planned my whole day to be spent at the passport office. And now I had a full day ahead with nothing to do. This kind of ridiculous efficiency is completely undemocratic. I spent the rest of the day wandering the streets of Mumbai muttering under my breath, 'I didn't even have the chance to take out my wallet and tell someone, "*Sir, jaldi se karva do na* [Sir, please hasten it up a bit],"' and slip two ₹100 notes in their hands. What was the point?

To be honest, I've lost track of my own sarcasm in this piece.

So, I'm just going to try and talk without irony.

Let's all take a breath and begin again...

India's corruption index has fallen in the recent years. And this is there to witness for thousands of Indians in different spheres. However, of the 180 countries in the ranking, we are ranked no. 86 in least corrupt.[13] There are other countries in the same ranking, we are in the esteemed company of China (hmmm), Benin (is that a sauce), Ghana (neighbours with Benin) and Morocco (definitely has a sauce). Indians can construe us being in the same company as China as a compliment, or an insult.

Countries that rank higher than us include Armenia, Suriname, Tunisia, Senegal, São Tomé and Príncipe (I seriously have no idea where that is), Greece (they have liquidity to bribe?) and Namibia, amongst others.

The problem is that bribery exists in many shapes and forms across the country. Here is a minor example: Mumbai roads.

If you live in Mumbai, you know our roads are spectacular and ensure careers of spine specialists, physiotherapists, gynaecologists and massage parlours. Either the cars in Mumbai have spikes in the wheels or the road quality is absolutely shit. Roads are built every day in Mumbai, all day.

I used to live in a place called Bandra West in Mumbai. It's one of the most expensive areas in the country and by that consequence in Asia. About 20 per cent of Bollywood elites live here, the remaining 80 per cent live in Versova where they try and cobble up a career so they can move to Bandra West.

Brokers in Bandra West are constantly telling you pitches like:

'Arrey, Sir. This house is right next to Ranbir Kapoor's

---

[13]PTI, 'India falls to 86th rank in corruption perception index 2020', *The Economic Times*, 28 May 2021, https://economictimes.indiatimes.com/news/economy/indicators/indias-rank-slips-to-86th-in-corruption-perception-index-2020/articleshow/80512814.cms. Accessed on 10 February 2022.

house. If you look out the window, sometimes you can see his car.'

I don't know who bases property decisions on being able to see Ranbir Kapoor's car, but there you have it.

I've also heard the following: 'Arrey, Sir. You know Aditya Pancholi? You know his son? One of his friends has a house down the road.'

I mentioned Bollywood elites and Aditya Pancholi in the same sentence, I know. Again: what kind of excitement exactly is garnered in buyers or renters with the possibility of seeing the son of a Bollywood star's best friend's house? What kind of uneventful life have you led?

Anyway, the area is a rich area. Salman, Shahrukh, Ranbir, etc., all have homes here. In case you were misled by the earlier Aditya Pancholi reference, some top business honchos and politicians also live here.

So, you'd expect the roads to not resemble an abandoned uranium mine. But, they do. Outside my house there was once a lane. And I mention it in the past tense because the lane used to exist, but then suddenly did not. And calling it a lane is a stretch because the road had more potholes in it than an actual road. One fine week, the municipality came and dug up the entire lane. The mud and rocks were piled up on one side, with the hole exposed. So, people that used to walk down the road were now given the option to go on a trek in the middle of the city or fill the hole with water and use gondolas to make their way across the Venetian lane.

This went on for two weeks. In the third week, they came and transferred the mud back to the hole. Then the fourth week came and they dug the hole. The fifth week they repaired the road. I use the word 'repaired' liberally, like you'd use the word 'sex' for a kiss. They found some rocks and stones from the beach and essentially just shoved them on the road.

Sure enough, the 'road' broke down in about three hours and stayed that way for a month. The same process was repeated thrice.

Now you ask me—er...Sorabh, what the living hell does all this have to do with bribery? And you know the answer—there's no way to prove this and no verifiable way to confirm this, but we all just assume that anywhere between some to all road contractors in India may be getting kickbacks to keep getting contracts, use inferior products and screw it up even more.

Normal people withdraw money from an ATM, contractors withdraw them from pretending to build roads. That road is a ledger account. And the credit side is the voting public. And, if it can exist in one of the richest parts of the city that is India's financial hub, you can be confident it stretches all over India.

Kickbacks, favours and/or corruption for infrastructure, government deals are a sad truth of any country, be it India, China, the US or even Europe. It's the lack of subtlety that is the issue in India. Our corruption is so blatant sometimes—it makes you question how stupid the authorities think we are.

While corruption in certain parts has been reducing, it's still an ailment in other parts. But, once again, your future Prime Minister has a solution.

## What Will I Do When I Become PM

A certain chief minister of a certain state that I won't name—because what I'm about to say is based on unverified rumours—apparently told contractors across the state, 'Since I can't stop corruption or bribery, here's the next best thing: I'll allow you guys to do it BUT you better finish the job you started. Or no booze for you. Actually, *and* no booze for you.'

What this allegedly did was improve completion rates of projects. If you can't change them, join them and make them finish their work.

I'd like to implement this as a nationwide concept. Legalize bribery, just call the act of doing it an 'upgrade'—much like we have economy and first class or general category and management quota or first class and second class or uber X and uber XL.

The method works like this: say you want to get a Voter ID. You can wait the standard six months, like I did. Or you can request an 'upgrade', where they have to deliver it within a month for ₹500 extra. Solved!

I see your doubts. And let me clear up all of them.

'This will lead to bureaucrats always asking for payments for any card or favour.' Yes, they may. May. But, for the most part, bureaucrats and netas already ask for payments for cards, work or favour. In this way, at least you have a receipt! It's tax-deductible corruption.

'This is elitist, democracy should not give you benefits just because you pay extra.'

Unfortunately, all democracies are weighed towards people that have extra money. If that wasn't the case, members of parliaments wouldn't increase their salaries every few years, without opposition.

'Why should we pay the government for things that are owed to us.'

Kindly read my chapter on taxes. However, these 'upgrades'

will also be on the basis of earning capacity. If you pay income tax, you pay ₹500. If you don't, you pay ₹499 (please pay income tax). If you can't afford to pay income tax, you pay ₹199. Next argument, please?

Also, I forgot to mention the most important part—inspired by the previously unnamed chief minister—if anyone takes money for an 'upgrade', in whichever sector and they do not complete the task assigned to them, they are executed in a public place. We will also play music praising Stalin as we do it.

While that's too extreme, I'm happy to settle with a punishment. And here it is: 100 years in jail. If you'd like to reduce your sentence to one day in jail, you have to pay ₹1 lakh to the person whose work you did not do. Solved! Also, seriously, we need to stop threatening to send people in jail for ridiculous crimes. Okay?

If you don't do the upgrade you were paid to do, then it's only fair that you directly upgrade the bank account of the person you denied the upgrade to.

I swear this is a genius solution and I should get at least three Bharat Ratnas for offering it. Thanks for giving me an upgrade of ₹295 to buy this book so that I can achieve my dreams of becoming a potometre.

## small thoughts

*It's always enjoyable when the government tries to catch up with technology and inevitably doesn't quite catch up. It's a variant of Moore's Law applied to government and technology. By the time they catch up, the technology has become two times better. A great case in point is the concept of free WiFi in certain parts of India—railway stations, bus stops, airports, etc.*

*The governments of the country spent a considerable amount of money on getting this done, but, by the time it was done, Mukesh bhai had made Internet so cheap, it was almost less expensive than free.*

*I'm sure this is elitism on my part and free WiFi benefits many people who can't access or afford mobile Internet. This list includes people who can't afford internet tariffs, travellers, young students (this has been proven by multiple news reports), small traders, etc. But, something tells me that a majority of people using this free WiFi are government officials trying to prove that free WiFi is a good idea. Because Mukesh bhai didn't make it affordable enough?*

*I'm relatively sure it's the latter because at one particular road where free Wifi was offered, I asked a friendly young labourer who was laying bricks if he used the free WiFi and he said, 'Itni ghatiya speed kisko chahiye, bhai? [Who needs such shitty Internet speed, bro?]'*

*P.S. I already redact the above statement because multiple stories have come from students and traders using this free WiFi. So, once again: I'm the idiot.*

# 5

# *Fraud: The Golden Ticket*

*Please note that while writing this chapter, I thought I was being a financial whiz and a version of Sucheta Dalal. I'm not. Most of this is based on information from the internet and I sound like a platypus trying to understand communism, or some idiot on the Internet trying to write a blog post of any kind.*

*So, take it with a pinch of salt. And, send me a bachelor's degree in Economics.*

There's a video of Vijay Mallya in London—walking with a beard shaped like a magician from Victorian times (his great trick is disappearing and then reappearing)—smoking a cigarillo as he walks toward the court for his hearing.[14] He waves to the media and answers their questions by saying, 'Good morning.'

'Do you think you'll be innocent?'

'Good morning.'

'Are you denying all charges.'

'Let the courts decide. Good morning.'

---

[14]'Undaunted Vijay Mallya appears in London court', *YouTube*, 12 January 2018 https://www.youtube.com/watch?v=6divBJKBo0Q. Accessed on 10 February 2022.

'Is it night time?'
'Good morning.'
'What do you say when someone you want to die, dies?'
'Good mourning.'
'What about banks?'
'Good borrowing.'

Obviously the last two are fake, but he reaches the court's steps, stubs the cigarillo on the ground and walks inside. It's the start of the magic trick. Where will Mallya appear after the courts? Maldives? Singapore? Moon? Will he have a twin brother?

The YouTube comments on this video are filled with people saying, 'Did he just stub a cigarette outside the courts? The fine for that is £80', 'Look at this man—will he pay the fine?' and 'Scamming a bank is another thing, but littering is worse', etc.

I saw the video, and I can't help but be mildly impressed by Vijay Mallya. Had I been in trouble over that amount of unpaid dues, I would have scampered to the court doors, picking up littered objects and putting them in dustbins to prove what a law-abiding citizen I am. Not Mallya. Mallya strolls the streets with the attitude of a man who thinks that all of London is part of his mansion in Goa.

There's plenty of Indians who have done scams in the past—businessmen, politicians, sportspersons, businessmen turned politicians, etc. But, no one seems quite as amusing as Vijay Mallya, even though there should be nothing amusing about a man who has unpaid debts in a developing country where income inequality is so severe.

The topic of Vijay Mallya may be a little bit more complicated than most Indians want to admit. A lot of us have a very simple response to it: 'Saala, chor. Mera personal paisa le ke bhaag gaya. Voh nahi hota toh main apne personal jet mein apne Maldives walle duplex mein FIFA World Cup host karta [Bloody thief. He took my personal money and ran away. Had he not been around, I would have been flying my personal jet to my duplex in Maldives and host the FIFA World Cup there.]'

The Vijay Mallya phenomenon is no longer about paying back loans, it's about what he represents. It's not about recovering money, it's about sending out a message to others in the future.

First off, this loan problem started when Kingfisher Airlines started back in 2005. Way back then, the airline was a major disruptor, despite suffering losses from the get-go. And, whose fault was it? Richard Branson.[15]

Branson's Virgin Airlines was a bit of a blueprint for Kingfisher Airlines, or so it seemed. The airline promised an exclusive flight experience for cheap. And to anyone except the customers, this cannot have been a suitable business model.

Mallya said that models would be hired as air hostesses, which has a few flaws: air hostesses are trained in being air hostesses, models are not. Also, models charge per assignment and considerably higher than the average air hostess (no offense intended) or even the average comedian (offense intended). Mallya said it would be a business class experience for an economy price, which has a few flaws: the reason business class costs more to buy is because it costs more to maintain. Pretty basic mathematics. As a promotional offer, yes, a great idea. As a business plan, a bit stupid?

---

[15] 'Why Vijay Mallya is not Richard Branson & vice versa', *The Economic Times*, 16 November 2011, https://economictimes.indiatimes.com/industry/transportation/airlines-/-aviation/why-vijay-mallya-is-not-richard-branson-vice-versa/articleshow/10708205.cms?from=mdr. Accessed on 2 March 2022.

An airline making losses is pretty normal for the first few years, but for an airline to not do due diligence and have a proper financial strategy before launching seems foolhardy. And it was. Imagine if your neighbour came to you and said, 'Hey. I have this business idea. I'm launching a bus service tomorrow. Each bus will have just 10 passengers, but they'll go in style from Pune to Bangalore. And we'll charge them just ₹235, the price of a state bus. Also, all our drivers will be trained hitmen who have spent 12 years with the Mossad. The cuisine will be caviar vada pav and free champagne. Do invest.'

What would your response be? Probably to block your neighbour's number, report him to Truecaller as spam and tell the residents' association that you're tired of living next to a psychopath.

Indian banks had the opportunity to do that with Kingfisher Airlines—yet, they sanctioned the loans. Yes, there is a possibility that aviation was trying to take off in India and maybe the industry was too new to understand what would work and what would not, but, if I were sanctioning loans up to (eventually) $1 billion, it's expected that you do some minor amount of research. Maybe they did, maybe they made a mistake.

At a minimum, you'd call up talent agents and ask them if they have any models and how much they'd charge for a gig on a plane. That answer (₹35,000 plus conveyance for me and six of my managers) itself would dissuade you from seeing $$$ signs or in this case ₹₹₹ signs in your eyes, let alone a repayment plan.

But, they did. With aplomb. Maybe they did the above, maybe they made a mistake.

Not only did Kingfisher Airlines lose money, it bought out another airline that was also not making money. Maybe they hoped for two negatives to make a positive. From the outset, it makes no sense, but in aviation sense, that is something that tends to be less obvious. Every airline in India that has acquired another airline has shut down soon after. It started when Ravana Air took over Pushpak.

(Now I know what the analysis of this joke would be: but, Sorabh, you ranting idiot, Pushpak was a private jet, at max. It was not an airline. Ravana did not have a fleet of Pushpaks flying from Colombo airspace to India and back, offering rakshasas discount offers to see enemy land. So, your joke makes no sense and kindly save it for the Indian Science Congress.)

Anyway, it got loans worth ₹6,900 crore from a consortium of 17 lenders in 2010.[16] I was once rejected a loan because I had taken one extra month to pay a credit card bill for ₹1,349. Mallya's persuasive powers are impressive, there is no doubt, to convince lenders that Kingfisher Airlines would make money. Either that, or there is something wrong with the system. It could also be both.

And obviously there is much wrong with the system as the CBI found out. I'm not sure and my incredible investigative journalism on Google (up to Page 3 of searches) has me confused of how many, if any, people were convicted.

While there is a high chance that I'm going down a path of cliché, it's surprising that no politicians have been arrested. It seems improbable that a loan for a struggling aviation sector company had not inched along even a bit without the behest

---

[16]PTI, 'CBI registers fresh case against Vijay Mallya', *Deccan Chronicle*, 13 August 2016, https://www.deccanchronicle.com/business/in-other-news/130816/beleaguered-liquor-baron-vijay-mallya.html. Accessed on 2 March 2022.

*Vote for Pant* ▪ 41

of a senior politician. Maybe they did the above, maybe they made a mistake.

But, that's never going to happen. Indian politicians are never guilty—they have scapegoats that are paid a lot to ensure that. This is not based on fact and is merely the assumption of many Indians—including my neighbours and relatives—and I provide this without any citations or references because I don't want to give their phone numbers. I exercise DND on their behalf.

Some things about this loan don't make sense to a lot of us, but makes sense for common practice at that time for issuing such loans. The assumption is that why did Mallya not attach any of his properties to this loan? It's the wrong question since that seems to be the case for most smart businessmen in India and abroad. So, the question of selling his property to pay off the loan is tenuous.

Now, here is where we come to the odd part. At its peak, Mallya owed Indian banks ₹9,100 crore. He offered to pay them ₹6,000 crore. [17] [18]

'What's a few thousand crores between friends? Come on banks, we've hung out at so many Diwali parties together; your loans and my kids go to the same schools. Be cool, banks. Be cool.'

---

[17] Vijayraghavan, Kala and Saloni Shukla. 'Vijay Mallya may make revised Rs 6,000 crore settlement offer to banks', *The Economic Times*, 14 April 2016, https://economictimes.indiatimes.com/news/politics-and-nation/vijay-mallya-may-make-revised-rs-6000-crore-settlement-offer-to-banks/articleshow/51817847.cms?from=mdr. Accessed on 15 February 2022.

[18] Vishwanath, Apurva. 'Vijay Mallya offers banks Rs 6,000 crore debt repayment plan', *Mint*, 31 March 2016, https://www.livemint.com/Politics/NHfg6BONdAluTYEizdJMhJ/Vijay-Mallya-submits-debt-repayment-plan.html. Accessed on 15 February 2022.

The banks refused and in the years succeeding that offer they have got nothing. So, you decide if it was the correct thing to do or not. And before you get on to a boat of outrage over it, read this: when Mallya offered this settlement, Indian banks were afraid of getting into trouble for accepting such a settlement with the CBI, the Central Vigilance Commission and others. Since 2017, the bankruptcy code has changed and allowed for such a settlement.[19]

It took us quite some time to figure out that getting a portion of a bad loan is better than getting nothing. While it's far from ideal, you'd prefer suffering losses of 20 per cent than suffering losses of 100 per cent. I learned that much doing my MCom.

It seems unfair that a big business would be allowed this option and why you, as a private individual, are not afforded the same right.

'Sorry, bank. I can't pay back the ₹20,000 loan for this scooter. Just take a haircut of ₹12,000 and let's move on. As a bonus, I'll let you ride pillion with me when you need to go to the market', is an approach that would unlikely work. But, businesses get precedence because they generate employment and taxes for many versus individuals who usually generate employment and taxes only for themselves.

I'm the guy on the scooter (I have a car. However, isn't a car two scooters with a roof?) However, the number of loans—and the sheer numbers of these loans—to big businesses are so significant that the numbers add up. Banks are more okay now

---

[19]'The Insolvency and Bankruptcy Code (Amendment) Bill', PRS Legislative Research 2017 https://prsindia.org/billtrack/the-insolvency-and-bankruptcy-code-amendment-bill-2017. Accessed on 2 March 2022.

than before to accept a loss on loans because they'd rather get back a few thousand crores so they can offer more loans for scooters than get back nothing and be unable to afford their own scooter. Yes, I am an esteemed economist and an idiot.

Such a situation is called a 'haircut' on loans—a last resort where a bank decides to settle a deal and take a loss in a one-time settlement when there is no hope for recovery. Allegedly, multiple Indian banks have taken a 'haircut' on loans worth ₹2.75 lakh crore from some big companies whose names you can search on Google.[20]

Mallya and his bad loans happened to fall outside the purview of these changes and there is a chance that he prompted it. So, all these 15 companies probably owe a debt (lol) to him for being one of the first defaulters to induce Indian banks to offer haircuts as a last resort.

It's not too late to do the same even now, but Mallya has become a symbol for politics.

A few weeks into the COVID-19 lockdown in India, rumours started flying that Vijay Mallya was going to be extradited to India. These rumours have been flying more prominently on WhatsApp than the death of Mr Bean—but, people happily believed them.

The comments under these rumours were always the same: '*Eh, Mallya. Yeh Congress ka time nahi hai, apna Modi hai—tu nahi bhaag paayega saale* [Eh, Mallya. This is not the time of the Congress, this is Modi's time—you won't be able to run away, thief].' And then there were just multiple comments

---

[20]Mathew, George. 'Banks write off Rs 2.02 lakh crore in FY21; Rs 10.7 lakh crore crore in last 7 years', *The Indian Express*, 13 December 2021, https://indianexpress.com/article/business/banking-and-finance/banks-write-off-rs-2-02-lakh-cr-in-fy21-7669513/. Accessed on 9 February 2022.

saying Modi, Modi, Modi, etc.

Given that kind of public response, the authorities are scarcely going to be forgiving to Mallya and forget a haircut on his loan, they'd be unlikely to pay for any kind of haircut, even without the shampooing.

The problem is what Mallya represents. First there's the alcohol—where some Indians still pretend that alcohol consumption is the most sinful of all activities until we need tax and until we need alcohol. The second is the Kingfisher calendar, the pomp, the glamour, the hoopla, the ridiculous yacht, the Goa villa and whatever else. The third is Mallya's 'swag' which is often interchangeable with shamelessness and correctly so.

For example, if you owe your country almost a billion dollars, you don't show up at an India cricket match in London (as Mallya did in the Champions Trophy in England) as if nothing has happened. You show up specifically to prove a point and tell people that you're a free bird, look at you.

(Indian cricketers apparently had to run for their lives at a function after that match upon realizing that Mallya would be coming there because that's a photo op that no one wants. Even if Virat was in a photo where he was breathing in the same air as Mallya, Indians would be like, '*Saala Virat. Tere lungs bhi desh drohi*? [Bloody Virat. Even your lungs are anti-national?]', because that's how crazy we sometimes are. If you owe salaries to your employees, you don't default and then rub your money in their faces.

If you're being tried for a court hearing, maybe, just maybe, you don't stub a cigarillo on the sidewalk.

Mallya has grown to represent something. And while all practicality dictates that giving him a haircut on his loans is/

was probably a good idea, emotionally, too many Indians are invested in the theme of the rich criminal getting away with it, again—as we've seen repeatedly.

I was talking to a friend and she pointed out a difference between Subrata Roy and Vijay Mallya, 'From a public perception, the difference between Subrata Roy and Vijay Mallya is that at least one spent time in jail.' From a public point of view, at least Roy 'paid' at the hands of justice, whereas Mallya has 'escaped' justice. Even though Roy targeted and scammed many poor Indians, at least he 'paid' for it.

Is it time for Indian banks to take a haircut on his loans and close this out? And I'm one to know about haircuts. But, once again as your official PM (Pant Man), I provide a workable solution: golden visas.

## What I'll Do When I Become PM

The reason Mallya is sitting in London is a golden visa, aka an investment visa, which the British government offers to people that can afford it. A golden visa is a visa issued by them and applicable even if your national passport is revoked. In essence, it is a permanent residency visa to individuals that invest in the country. The list includes Tiger Hanif (accused in the Gujarat bomb blasts of 1993), Nadeem Saifi (accused of conspiring against Gulshan Kumar for his murder), Nirav Modi, Lalit Modi, various questionable Russians and Chinese names that you can Google unless they've been erased from all memory. And before you think, 'Oh that's great, let's do a couple of scams in India and then go chill in the UK,' please hold your horses. Because UK is not your only option. Expand your horizons, you ambitious scamster. These visas are offered by many countries. So, explore your travel options before you commit scams. Don't be hasty, the world is your oyster if you're rich. You may also explore immigrant investor programmes in about 21 rich countries.

Here's how a golden visa works: you have to agree to invest £2 million into the British economy over a five-year period, i.e. about ₹20 crore.[21] If you'd like—I'm sure some bank may be willing to loan you that amount—just ask around.

It also raises questions about where a Tiger Hanif (aide of Dawood Ibrahim) and Nadeem got that kind of cash, but that's another story.

Since 2015, 58 Indians have applied for this visa.[22] Three of them have already been named in the last few pages. That's, at a minimum, 10 per cent of applicants with questionable backgrounds, though that number may be higher. So, if you commit a crime, don't call a lawyer, first call your travel agent and after you're settled in, then call a lawyer.

It's obviously not as easy as it used to be: Roshni Kapoor, daughter of Yes Bank co-founder, Rana Kapoor, who was accused of fraud worth ₹4,300 crore, was stopped from flying to London at Mumbai airport.[23] So, please make your travel plans early. Pre-book flights abroad and then fly.

---

[21]Shukla, Srijan. 'What is "golden visa" to UK that Indians are spending £2 million on', *The Print*, 28 February 2020, https://theprint.in/theprint-essential/what-is-golden-visa-to-uk-that-indians-are-spending-2-million-on/372857/. Accessed on 9 February 2022.
[22]Ibid.
[23]Rajput, Rashmi and Jaikishan Yadav. 'ED arrests Yes Bank founder Rana Kapoor; daughter stopped at Mumbai International Airport', *The Economic Times*, 9 March 2020, https://economictimes.indiatimes.com/news/politics-and-nation/ed-arrests-yes-bank-founder-rana-kapoor-daughter-stopped-at-mumbai-international-airport/articleshow/74539869.cms?from=mdr. Accessed on 4 March 2022.

A golden visa helps some of the above—Mallya, Tiger Hanif, Nirav Modi, etc.,—each time India asks for their extradition and UK courts rule against it citing the bad/horrible state of Indian jails. Because '*atithi devo bhava* [guest is god]', especially one that's invested ₹20 crore.

This kind of situation also allows the British government to have a bargaining chip and gain political clout and they're not alone in offering it. St Kitts and Nevis—an island country in the West Indies—was one of the first to offer this option in 1984.[24] Since then it has caught on and is offered (with genuine intent of investments by the countries, misused often by those escaping criminal charges) by the UK, Malta, Cyprus, Canada, Spain, Grenada, USA, Turkey, Australia, HK, Singapore, UAE and many others.

The UK granted 255 golden visas in the first half of 2019 alone[25]—that's half a billion pounds just off immigration! I'm not judging, I'm just impressed. Why is India not offering the same? And also can someone lend me ₹20 crore?

Here's what we must do: golden, silver, bronze, platinum visas. Why stop at golden visas, let's take the next step.

## *Golden Visa*

If you invest $2 million in India, you become an Indian citizen and every year you get one high-five from the Prime

---

[24] Semotiuk, Andy J. 'St Kitts And Nevis Possibly An Investor Immigrant's Best 2nd Passport', *Forbes*, 17 August 2020, https://www.forbes.com/sites/andyjsemotiuk/2020/08/17/st-kitts-and-nevis-possibly-an-investor-immigrants-best-2nd-passport/?sh=255268363a61. Accessed on 15 February 2022.

[25] Neate, Rupert. 'Rise in number of world's rich buying UK "golden visas"', *The Guardian*, 27 September 2019, https://www.theguardian.com/uk-news/2019/sep/27/number-of-foreigners-buying-uk-golden-visa-rises. Accessed on 15 February 2022.

Minister. Plus, a season pass to the IPL (unless it happens outside India—in every aspect of your situation, you must pay for your own flights).

### Silver Visa

Invest $1.5 million in India, you get Permanent Residency (PR) and the President of India gives you a low-five. Plus, season pass for Kabaddi Premier League (it's a good league).

### Bronze Visa

Invest $1 million. You get PR and the Vice President of India follows you on Twitter. Plus, season pass for Indian Idol (do they have passes: who knows?)

### Platinum Visa

Invest whatever you're due (or haircut). This is offered to Indians accused of crimes and who took the golden visa in the UK. You get PR (Permanent Residency) and PR (Public Relations). You pay off what you can in loans, face the courts and you have to spend one year being screamed at during Indian debates.

The money earned from these visas can be invested in improving the state of the Indian jails, which is anyway a good thing, and also eliminates the defense of bad state of Indian jails.

Solved. All hail me. And give me that bank loan. Or citizenship.

# 6

# *How to Use Motivational Speakers to End Unemployment (of Motivational Speakers)*

*'What human beings CAN do is truly amazing, isn't it? But what people WILL do is usually disappointing...'*

—Tony Robbins, summarizing my career

Unemployment rates in India have reached ridiculous figures. Experts say the per cent is going to hit double digits or have already hit double digits, but definitely not triple digits. Now, I don't know what any of that means, but it sounds like a lot. I personally know so many people that have had to improvise and find new avenues to make money: writing books, earning money from Super Chat on YouTube and begging brands to treat them like an influencer and send them free stuff, so they can re-sell it to friends in their building. This might all be one person.

But, seriously: it's devastating and tragic and terrible. And much worse for plenty of people who are struggling to make ends meet. And I don't know what realistic advice or hope to give to people surviving on the brink, so let me delve once more into the fantasy world of outlandish comedy that completely circumvents anything feasible. I believe that's how you campaign.

On YouTube, there are two kinds of advertisements I constantly come across: first, there are the ones asking people to donate money to those in need. Those advertisements pull at your heart strings because you don't have money even for yourself. But, okay fine, here's my fourth donation of the week, and there comes more advertisements for more such donations. Great.

The second is ads for motivational speakers, to help you earn extra income to donate to the above. And there are also motivational speakers telling you how to start your own business (which is a great idea during the pandemic), how to be a better employee (which people are trying their best to be, so they don't lose the job they are holding on to with dear life) and a better person (who has the time, we're all trying to make money and bam—I've put on six kilograms more this week).

This whole piece may sound extremely bitter and that's because it is very bitter. As a comedian, I have encountered motivational speakers at corporate shows and been shown my place around them. People look at motivational speakers as humans that can change your life and spread positivity with just a touch (much like COVID-19). Motivational speakers will tell you the world is great and you can be anything, and comedians are telling you that it's definitely not and you certainly won't. And the difference between that is definitely one zero in the cheque. In one particular instance, I was told the motivational speaker earned two zeros more than me plus an extra digit on the side, which was apparently more than the price of the entire event.

So, if I sound bitter and sadistic towards the profession, please note that I sincerely mean it.

I've seen some great motivational speakers. One man, who played drums and got a group of people to break a dahi-handi onstage while the whole crowd clapped and danced and had a ridiculous amount of positivity, screamed at them. Another who spoke about embracing failure, and another who was more than capable of giving tremendous comebacks to everyone.

Then there are others who show up to talk about how they have a really great car and you can too without really telling you how (one extra zero), or another whose entire spiel was about quoting other people's motivational quotes and saying how they were great, or still another who was such a horrible motivator that three people in the crowd went to sleep. This was before lunch, which is honestly a tremendous achievement.

So, I know some are superb at their job and the deluge of it is interesting. And I know people feel that way about comedians as well but, I've never had a great opinion of us comedians—so, it all balances out.

Like many people, the first motivational book I read was *How to Win Friends & Influence People* by Dale Carnegie. The advice was simple: call people by their first name, smile, look at people's interests and make them feel important, sincerely. One of the only things I remember is calling people by their first name and it's the reason for my success and the billions of dollars I have stacked in all three of the islands in Cayman.

There are some fantastic motivational speakers out there, but most of them roughly say the same things in their videos that Carnegie wrote about, added with a few things:

- *Wake up early.* Now this is a great advice. But, no one tells you how to wake up early when you have kids and also want to drink and also want to take a walk with your wife and also want to spend three hours stalking people on Instagram. But, they'll say, 'Wake up early. I woke up today at 3.00 a.m. for my day tomorrow so I can get a head start on next week.' Great, happy for you, you bird. Next.
- *Talk to and be interested in other human beings.* The biggest flaw in this is that this involves talking and being interested in other human beings. Next.
- *Invest in yourself.* I have kids. I'm investing in their school fees. Next.
- *Say yes to opportunities and learn them later.* That's how I had kids. Next.
- *Network every day.* I have kids. No time. Next.
- P.S. I just realized that I have kids. So none of this makes sense for me. Next to all.

A lot of it is basic common sense and a lot of it is nonsensical platitudes. One technique the modern motivational speaker uses is to list a bunch of popular, famous names and then find a connection. It's such an old technique, I can't believe it still works.

'Bill Gates. Elon Musk. Albert Einstein. Steve Jobs. Warren Buffett. Jack Ma. Larry Page. Richard Branson. Mahatma Gandhi. Larry Ellison. Kim Jong-un. Mukesh Ambani. Mark Zuckerberg. Pol Pot. Vijay Shekhar...what do they all have in common? They're all carbon-based life forms and if you sign up for my two-day $35,000 seminar, you can be one too.'

And people will sign on because carbon makes diamonds and we all want to be De Beers.

Another YouTube speaker offered a 10-day course to people to start their own business online and this is what he said:

- The sessions are pre-recorded so you can watch them anytime. (Because I don't want to have to say this stuff more than once.)
- In Session 1, we will explain to you how to start up your own domain name for your business. (There's about 12,000 websites that offer this service and also starting your business with the name first is a really refreshing and ridiculous idea. Hi, my business is called RazorBlast. Oh wow, what does it do? I don't fucking know, that's Session 2.)
- In Session 2, we will explain how you can procure goods from buyers and source it via your website. (Sounds like a flawless plan by Jeff Bezos in 1994.)
- In Session 3, we will teach you how to connect to industry leaders using online websites. (So, basically LinkedIn. You're showing people where LinkedIn is located.)

And apparently, over 10,000 people signed on for the course, meaning LinkedIn had 10,000 new accounts that month.

One speaker offered a course in teaching people public speaking, but for some strange reason he spoke in an affected American accent. I don't want to make fun of people's accents unless they're intentionally fake and his was because he kept slipping in and out of it, almost as if he had watched a video on how to do public speaking in America and was copy-pasting it. The man should know that American accents don't induce people to follow you, British accents do. That even works in America. That's how colonialism started. Before trade and guns and slavery, there was the accent. Take notes.

But my point is this: my favourite advertisement for motivational speakers is the one telling people that they can learn from this motivational speaker on how to become one too. First lesson, do not opt for the course.

And I know that eventually I will 100 per cent be offering a course on how to become a comedian. And I suggest you take that course because if I'm doing that course it means I *really* need the money and/or someone has kidnapped a member of my family and the only way out is to do the course. The third reason could be that I've just given up.

The idea, however, is terrific and can ease out unemployment—just having people learn how to become motivational speakers and teach others too. This would lead to an endless number of people motivating each other. It'll be a great world—maybe it will be disguised unemployment, but at least we'll all feel good about ourselves. We'll feel motivated to motivate.

Thousands or lakhs of Indians can create this system and I know you think that sounds like a pyramid scheme—that's exactly and precisely what I want it to be. Isn't everything a pyramid scheme waiting to collapse?

I'm not a financial analyst. In fact, I've never even done the first four letters of the word 'analyst'. But, that qualifies me to talk about anything because it's my book. Here's my theory: everything is a pyramid scheme waiting to collapse.

A pyramid scheme is where you recruit people to recruit other people, without really supplying any kind of product.

The banking system or even cryptocurrency or even being a sports fan—it's all a pyramid scheme. Please let me know when I should become the RBI governor, I've cracked it.

Of course, the ultimate pyramid scheme is religion, and the afterlife is where you truly discover that there's really nothing at the top of the pyramid. Or maybe not. But, let's not go there. I respect your faith and belief.

Pyramid or ponzi schemes have devastated people's lives. Millions and billions of dollars have been lost. One day, we can be as great as Albania almost was. Yes, I said such words. Now this is not an affront on Albania or India—both are great countries. One I know by experience, one I'm giving a benefit of doubt.

But, in 1997, there was a horrible civil war in Albania which led to 2,000 people dying—all at the back of a pyramid scheme worth $1.2 billion dollars (I think that's a little more than Mallya's debts or Trump's once unpaid taxes—but, then Albania has a population one-fifth of Mumbai and hence, the demographics). A country was almost destroyed over a pyramid scheme.[26] And if you think a country in scale is different than a person, then please get to know about Bernie Madoff, who was given prison for life for a fraudulent pyramid scheme that was worth $64.8 billion dollars.[27] That's 60 times the scheme in Albania. Because one American can be more ambitiously

---

[26]Jarvis, Christopher. 'The Rise and Fall of Albania's Pyramid Schemes', International Monetary Fund, March 2000, https://www.imf.org/external/pubs/ft/fandd/2000/03/jarvis.htm. Accessed on 16 February 2022.

[27]'Bernie Madoff died in prison after carrying out the largest Ponzi scheme in history—here's how it worked', *Business Insider*, 15 April 2021, https://www.businessinsider.in/finance/news/bernie-madoff-died-in-prison-after-carrying-out-the-largest-ponzi-scheme-in-history-heres-how-it-worked/articleshow/82072614.cms. Accessed on 2 March 2022.

fraudulent than an entire country.

What all this tells me is not that the pyramid schemes will eventually destroy you, it shows that none of these fools have done a pyramid scheme properly. And I believe we can.

I believe the Indian people are the greatest people in the world. And with my course on how motivational speakers can make other people motivational speakers till every Indian house has at least one motivational speaker motivating the speakers of their house to become motivational speakers, we can truly get motivated and fight unemployment.

And if you think that's a bad idea, it's definitely better than trying to increase employment by hiring psychos from across the country to spread hate and mistrust on social media for between ₹3–15 per tweet or WhatsApp messages. This is based on an assumption through a WhatsApp message.

Most of those people don't even know how to call you by your first name.

Solved. No other solution needed.

## small thoughts

*I was speaking to this sweet kid in my building who innocently asked why her nanny did not speak English. I told her to ask how many languages her nanny speaks.*

*The nanny laughed and replied, 'Hindi, Marathi, Telugu and a little bit of Kannada and Tamil.'*

*I told the little girl she should be asking us why we speak only two languages.*

*And while this sounds like the kind of fake story a politician will spread to pretend they're relatable, it actually happened.*

*And I find this constant judgement towards people not speaking a language or not speaking it well quite tiring. The whole point of language is communication; when you judge someone or get abusive or aggressive over someone not speaking a language—whichever one it may be—maybe the only thing you're communicating is how you're not the best person.*

*P.S.: Making fun of friends' language (as with everything else) is a different thing...*

# 7

# *Population: Not My Problem!*

I want to start by congratulating all of us Indians—us, our parents, our grandparents—for having the sheer number of unprotected sex that we did. We may not be beating China in other departments (despite what misguided nationalists might tell you), but we are living it up in manufacturing people. For every phone that China makes, India makes two people—every product needs two consumers to induce demand and supply.

India's population is a massive problem. And, no one talks about it. No politician ever acknowledges it. Because Indians tend to be stupidly emotional about everything. If a politician says 'population is too much', some Indians think, 'Why does he hate me? I am also part of the population. Bastard.'

Additionally, when another kid is born, netas don't see that as population. They see vote bank. The second that kid pops out, they go: 'Vote for us. Caesarean section you came out? We do surgical strikes as well! Come on, baby!' or 'Vote for the other us. Our progress also continues because of being born', or 'Vote for the both of us. We both believe in dynasty despite all denial.'

Politicians keep saying, 'Our population is our strength.' That is their way of saying, 'We don't know what to do to control it!'

It's one of the two sections in India that gets a free pass for all its actions: religion (the other being politics). Fundamentalists of religion seem to want to create babies, sometimes citing religious conquest as a reason to make more babies, especially to those not educated enough to know that raising two good kids is better than raising a cricket team of dumbasses.

They feed on the insecurity of some people. Extremists will tell people to have more kids so as to compete with another religion, because their population must not make us extinct, even though, few mainstream religions have the problem of under population. Why do you need so many more humans? God forbid (or gods—whatever makes you happy) a holy war breaks out—you can't use humans as ammunition. First of all, that's morally horrific and second, humans are soft.

We come with historical issues. You know when people used to need to have six to 10 kids when we were solely an agrarian society? To help with the crops, you needed more hands. Plus the infant mortality rate was so high that you needed concussion substitutes for your kids. Spare batteries in the drawer.

Now, you don't! The infant mortality rate is much lower, plus technology exists. Plus you have other jobs. You don't need nine kids, you need two good kids. Even, one good kid will do. Like my parents had: my sister.

In the past, you ask your grandmoms and they'd say, '*Haan, humare 25 bacche the, 22 kab paida huye pata hi nahi chala* [Yes, we had 25 kids, we don't realize when were the 22 born].'

My grandmom had five kids, which was conservative by those standards. It was mainly because my granddad passed away early; please don't accuse her of not competing. She used to tell me of a friend who had 11 kids. '*11 bacche the, ek ghum gaya* [There were 11 children, one was lost].' Lost. Not in birth or something. Just lost the child. Like the child was a purse or a mobile phone. Please check behind the sofa, maybe in your purse?

This lady used to send all 11 kids out to play, so what she did was—she'd tie a string on all of them. Release them outside the house. When it was time for lunch, she'd pull them back, like they were fish and the world outside was a pond.

I'm so much nicer to both my kids. I feel great as a parent. I have never tied a string on them to bring them back, except that one time we were play-acting Baa Baa Black Sheep.

That same lady had her first kid when she was 14—14. At 14, I was in class IX, studying Biology. This lady was doing biology.

But, her story was in the 1950s and while I don't have a calculator, we can't have a version of the same attitude (use your calculator) years later.

Two kids are good. Biologically it matches. You have two breasts—one to feed each. You have two testicles—one to provide seed for each. This is basic science. And, yes, I failed in science.

The Indian population is a colossal problem. Sometimes, I wish we had a zombie apocalypse. I dream of it. Not because I want the end of civilization, but because I really am sick of waiting in line for train tickets. I wish if there was an attack, I'd be able to board the fast train on time for once.

And this is my commitment to India—if I'm one of the first to get bitten in a zombie apocalypse, that's okay. I'm happy to pave the way for someone else to catch their train, for I am a team player.

P.S.: I know that it's a weird time to even suggest an event that would wipe out a large number of people. I am aware.

China had their much disputed one-child policy—upgraded to a two-child policy in 2016—where fines were charged for anyone having more than the number of sanctioned kids.[28] The story obviously came with considerable issues attached, but we need a variation of the same in India. Do a tax rebate! Anyone with two or less kids, gets a 1 per cent tax deduction. We need this. Because, I have two kids. Sorry. They're already made.

We need more family planning in India. We need more people to know about vasectomies, which by the way is now a reversible process. Theoretically, you can get it on Tuesday, get it reversed on Thursday. Like curling and straightening your hair—but slightly more complicated. Now, obviously you can't do exactly that—but the point stands. Or doesn't. Depending on what is standing. I'm no doctor.

It's not a big deal. But, most Indians don't know it. Because, we don't think vasectomy, we think NASBANDI. And that word has all these connotations from back in 1970s, when Indira Gandhi's son, Sanjay Gandhi, ran a forced sterilization programme. While India needed a sterilization campaign, we did not need to be forced. Otherwise we are not a democracy.

His implementation was wrong, intention was right. It was the Congress' demonetization. Except the withdrawals

---

[28]'China allows three children in major policy shift', *BBC News*, 31 May 2021, https://www.bbc.com/news/world-asia-china-57303592. Accessed on 15 February 2022.

were considerably more painful. Things were so bad at that time—apparently, government doctors had to convince two men to do a NASBANDI every month. If they couldn't, they were fined a portion of their salary. I'm just imagining doctors running around, '*Yaar tu decide kar, ya toh tera katega, ya mera* [You decide, either yours will get cut, or mine].'

And, I know simplistically saying something gets 'cut' proves that I'm not a doctor—and that's okay because I'm not. I will be, once I start my own universities, but that's for later. Dr Sorabh Pant, neurologist of Ben Cutting.

Vasectomies should come with a payment attached. Every time you get a vasectomy or a tubectomy, you get ₹5,000. If the government thinks that's a lot of money, that's the money saved in taking care of one more person. Rupees five thousand is less than the money you'd spend as a government on taking care of an extra person.

It's just rewards for not adding another child we can't afford. If a couple gets a vasectomy and a tubectomy, even better—that's ₹12,000. Best offer. Like buying burgers and getting fries free—gynaecologists and urologists are losing their mind reading these comparisons, which makes me happy.

Twelve thousand rupees is a lot of money. But, I'll make it even better. If the parents choose to use that money to finance the education of their existing child, the government will instead pay ₹25,000 toward that child's education. I will term this initiative the Sterilization Scholarship.

Here's the public service advertisement for the same:

Man walks into his local kiraana shop. The owner gives him a smile, puts onions in his bag, he smiles back at her and then at the onions.

Kiraana shop owner (KSO): 'Did you hear? Rita got a ₹25,000 scholarship for her BTech.'

Man: 'Really? I didn't know she was that intelligent. She once asked me whether hyenas like jokes and if that's why they laugh.'

KSO: 'No, no. She's really an idiot. She has four accounts on TikTok just so she can get three likes on each. But, her parents just got permanent contraception to make Rita more intelligent.'

Man: 'Arrey, what a great idea. My son, Sanju is also an idiot. I will apply for this immediately.'

KSO: 'Of course, you should. I got a tubectomy and my husband got a vasectomy. We are hoping our son, Dimbu, also learns Java.'

Then a VO by Amitabh Bachchan plays, as KSO and Man nod to camera, smiling holding onions:

> *'Baccho ko banao aur buddhiman,*
> *Agar aap ho man ya woman*
> *Abhi apnaiye Sterilization Scholarship*
> *Taaki aapke bacche na rahe dumb as shit.'*

[Make your kids smarter
Whether you're a man or a woman
Apply for the Sterilization Scholarship
So your kids don't remain dumb as shit.]

I await my Abby Award and my election.

I think it's a great initiative, but I believe in it half-heartedly because of this story. My mom told me once, 'We never planned you, you just came.' So, if my own plan was implemented, I may never have been born to talk about this. I snuck through the border. I'm an illegal immigrant in life.

As I already said: I'm a team player and I'm happy to not even be born as long as my ideas are.

One other reason we may have such shitty family planning: condoms. Indians have sexualized condoms so much. Every condom ad is just soft porn. It's two horny people writhing and rubbing against each with more lust than the last pair of humpback whales. So, an Indian society that anyway denies sex as a natural act and has prudishness in-built into our system sees this and thinks, '*Chee, chee*. What are these people doing? Disgusting. I'd rather be Neena Gupta in *Badhaai Ho* than go through this.' Condoms prevent a result of sex—but they don't have to constantly show sex to indicate towards the worst outcome of the act (joke). Ads for cars don't show cars crashing into each other, those for Hajmola don't show piles of faeces, those for soap don't show hair stuck on the soap after bath.

We really can't keep sexualizing condoms so much even though it's about sex. Young people of India don't particularly care anymore, but the prudes that do are also the same that make excessive babies. For them we need to realign how condom ads are made.

They need to communicate condoms as a practical thing, as if they're advertising Life Insurance. I just imagine someone that everyone trusts—the great and my favourite actor, late Irrfan Khan. Him just sitting on a couch talking:

'*Chaudah crore bacche ho gaye. Aur kitne banaoge? Bhav maalum hai baccho ka? Ek bacche ke liye 1 crore rupay zindagi bhar gawaaoge tum. Paisa bachao. Soch lo. Ek crore ya 20 rupay ka Moods condom. Much better idea, na?* [1.4 million kids are already there. How many more do you need? Do you know how much kids cost? 1 kid costs approximately 1 crore rupees. Save your money. Think about it. One crore rupees or ₹20 worth Moods Condom. A better idea, right?]'

It's perfect.

P.S.: If you're one of those psychos that thinks that the joke is 'offensive' to the memory of Irrfan Khan, he tweeted about a similar joke I made about him and and not only found it funny but added his own joke to it. This is why Irrfan Khan remains someone I love and if you're offended, you should learn from him. And maybe put some kind of contraceptive to prevent your mind from being offended.

## What I'll Do When I Become PM

While India is overpopulating and China is also pretending not to—other countries are struggling. Japan has a decline in population. This is an opportunity for us. When we hear a country like some European nation or Japan with a declining populations, we think, 'How is such a thing even possible? Declining population? Is half your nation samurais of pulling out—what?'

Japan is struggling to create enough people. We can help. I offer them this: take some of our people. We will teach them Japanese. Most Indians are trilingual, if not bilingual. One more language will not make a difference. We will also train these Indians to assimilate into Japanese culture by teaching them manners and social customs, even if that restricts the number of cities we can send Indians from. I'm not naming the cities.

Japan, you can try 20 of our Indians as a sample size. We will base it on our demographics: take 16 Hindus, three Muslims and one person who is Christian, Sikh and Buddhist—Parwinder D'Souza Ashoka (is that a name?) Many Indians, anyway, have ambitions of leaving India—this just legitimizes it and makes their dreams come true as well as resolve the problems of other nations. Everyone wins.

If it all works out, we can start sending people to all countries reeling under declining birth rates. Japan, Bulgaria, Moldova, Serbia, Latvia, Lithuania—we will help you all out. There are other countries too with declining populations—but, no one wants to go there, so I won't name you personally, Serbia.

Elon Musk wants to send people to Mars. I want to send Indians to the rest of the world. Countries, please note: India will export our favourite product: people. Our citizens are working towards production as we speak.

## *small thoughts*

*Paraphrasing what Neil deGrasse Tyson once said, it would be easier to make the Earth liveable than trying to colonize Mars. And if that logic holds true, it raises the question: what is really the point of trying to colonize Mars?*

*And I think we all know the answer: it's the fear of the first person that will press the red nuclear bomb button.*

*Currently, the nuclear bomb is not too far from a Taliban, milder religious fundamentalists, an unpredictable dictator as well as another dictator in disguise (take your pick as to who that could be). Anything could happen and the impending domino effect of nuclear bombs could plough down Earth.*

*So, let's head to Mars, and escape the button of the psychos— also for human reasons of science, discovery, advancement and more.*

*P.S.: It would be tragic and also kind of hilarious if the next nuclear attack happens on Mars, decimating the years of work done by the first settlers.*

# 8

## *Air India Sold!*

Air India was started as Tata Airlines in October 1932. The government has been trying to sell it since November 1932. Even before we got independence from the British, the Indian government has been talking about selling their national airline. It was one of the things the British and Indians agreed on, the urge to sell our national carrier. And every month since November 1932, the government has extended the deadline for the sale. It extended the sale deadline for Air India (in all its avatars) by two months, 516 times.

While none of the above is true, it sounds true especially since the government actually took over Air India in 1953. It sounds so plausible. Because talks of selling Air India has been going on since I started flying in 1988—maybe I caused it. The first flight I ever flew in was Air India—Delhi to Mumbai. Maybe seeing me on the plane caused the government to rethink having a state airline.

'If people like that are flying, we really shouldn't be in this business', was an official statement from then aviation minister, Icarus Patil, after I landed in Mumbai.

The reason the government has been trying to sell Air India is because it's not been profitable for years. That is honestly ironic. The government(s) has a fractured relationship with aviation in India. On one end, they want to support flying so that more Indians can fly, and on the other end, they tax it to a point where making profit is almost impossible.

Think of the number of Indian airlines that have gone bust or have had to get a bailout from the government to survive. And it's not as if the number of flyers reduced. SpiceJet was on the verge of shutting down while being one of the most popular airline in the country![29] That is ridiculous.

You'd think the government would realize that it's their policies and taxes that push airlines to the brink—since the airline they manage is almost unmanageable. But, no, logic in front of taxation is a tough challenge for logic to win.

Here's something to prove the above point—IPL teams versus airlines. Owning a team at the IPL is not exactly like burning money. But, it's close. It's like taking crores of rupees and putting them in an open bag in a public place in Ghaziabad, hoping to make a profit. It took IPL teams eight years of being in the IPL to turn a profit. Eight years! And this does not include the IPL teams that sunk after two years—because their open bag was raided in one season.

But, here's the point: Royal Challengers Bangalore (RCB) started in 2008 and made a profit in 2018—which amounted to more than 10 per cent of the operating profit of United Spirits, the owners of RCB.[30]

---

[29]Makwana, Bhakti. 'Indigo stock gains as a plea to shut down SpiceJet has been admitted', *Business Insider India*, 8 December 2021, https://www.businessinsider.in/stock-market/news/indigo-stock-gains-as-a-plea-to-shut-down-spicejet-has-been-admitted/articleshow/88138734.cms. Acccessed on 9 February 2022.

[30]Malviya, Sagar. 'United Spirits earns over 10% of operating profit from cricket in FY19', *The Economic Times*, 7 June 2019, https://economictimes.indiatimes.com/industry/cons-products/liquor/united-spirits-earns-over-10-of-operating-profit-from-cricket-in-fy19/articleshow/69684044.cms. Accessed on 2 March 2022.

It doesn't take a genius to figure this out, so let me:

- RCB has never won an IPL title, but is now more than profitable. Kingfisher was seemingly at the top of Indian aviation for a couple of years, but now doesn't really exist.
- The BCCI is more generous with profits than the Indian government.
- Both the aviation league and the cricket league have been plagued by an equal number of scams.
- Except in aviation, the scams have been so momentous that three of India's biggest businessmen were embroiled or convicted in criminal cases. IPL had just two—on a minor scale in comparison.

Cricket in India (with all its dominion of profit-makers) is more profitable than operating with the government. Quite incredible.

Air India could be more profitable if it had an IPL team—the Air Indian Jamshedpur team may have turned a profit before the airline.

But, let's explore the airline itself.

A massive problem for Air India has been mismanagement. Because, politicians should not be running airlines—they have a history of barely running states and cities. A pilot told me that apparently every aircraft for Air India has 450 employees, compared to Indigo which has 70. That's 380 extra people hanging out? Is this a political rally? Where there's some important people and the rest are just an entourage to make it seem grander than the reality?

It's a tough job for a government to run airlines. There are good airlines across the globe that are government owned—this is on the basis of an in-depth study conducted by the aviation magazine *Uddta Pant,* based on my personal experiences flying all over the world: Singapore Airlines (they once had a connecting flight cancelled and put us up, all-expenses paid, at a five-star hotel for one day. I was hoping the next flight also got delayed), Emirates, Malaysia, Druk Air (Bhutan's small airline that flies you through a verdant valley while landing into a gorgeous airport—what's not to love?), but it's a tough task to have bureaucrats make profits in an industry that works on ridiculously tight margins.

Here's an example from me as an economist.

Jet Airways had to shut down while Indigo did not. What is the difference between the two? Sabudana khichdi on sale for ₹150.

Since I'm a nerd with no work, I attempted to calculate this difference. Indigo sells food on the airline, Jet used to give it for free. Now, Indigo has 1,500 daily flights (pre-COVID). The capacity of a flight is 180, the average number of seats is 100. Of these 100 people, about 30 are perpetually hungry like me. The average purchase per person is ₹200. That's ₹6,000 per flight on food, multiplied by 1,500 daily flights. That's 90 lakh earnings from food, daily. The profit margin is apparently 50 per cent, so, Indigo may have been making ₹45 lakh per day just by selling sabudana khichdi. Over 13 years. That's a profit of ₹2,100 crore on sabudana khichdi.

Sabudana khichdi has not made those kinds of profits across all Navratras in Gujarat in 10 years!

Even if you adjust these numbers to the following factors—Indigo's ATR planes (74 seats) or the number of flights per day being less before 2019 or the fact that I'm an idiot and only did my MCom—that's still at least ₹1,000 crore on just selling food.

By the same calculation, Jet Airways was giving people free food. Each meal would have cost ₹150 (conservatively) and on the basis of this calculation, that's an additional cost across 13 years of about ₹10,000 crore. Even if you half this amount on the basis of me being an idiot who doesn't understand Math—that's ₹5,000 crore, at least.

So, the difference between Jet Airways and Indigo just on the basis of sabudana khichdi, lukewarm samosa and black coffee for ₹100 is ₹6,000 crore.

Jet Airways has accumulated debt of nearly ₹8,500 crore on its books with total liabilities of around ₹25,000 crore.[31]

You want to know how tight the margins of success versus failure of an airline are? There it is: the difference is the announcement, 'Patrons, we will be starting the sale of food and beverages after take-off.' That announcement is worth an airline shutting down or not.

Compare that to Air India. Meals are free on most sectors. For years and years and decades. And sometimes, so are the seats. Every time I've been on the airline, the flight is 'sold out' or close to full. And if you ask the person sitting next to you, they will tell you that they have a government job or got discounted fares. It's pretty hard to make a profit if (arguably) 25 per cent of your seats are not for profit.

This increases jet fuel used and all the additional factors related to handling more people. You don't have to be an

---

[31] Rebello, Joel and Saloni Shukla, 'Decision on Jet Airways course likely today', *The Economic Times*, 17 June 2019, https://economictimes.indiatimes.com/industry/transportation/airlines-/-aviation/decision-on-jet-airways-course-likely-today/articleshow/69818927.cms?from=mdr. Accessed on 3 March 2022.

aviation economist (like me) to understand this is not a profitable model.

Now look, I've had some wonderful flights with Air India (the Dreamliner, for example) but, the proportion of not good flights is significantly high. Like the time my food tray was broken and I was told, 'What to do? It's only two hours,' which is weirdly reassuring.

But, free seats and free food and overstaffed airline do not make a profit!

Air India is also the flight I've had weird fights in, probably because of the same reason. I was sitting in the window seat and if you sit in the window seat (which you've paid for) you own the window. It's your dominion. You've paid ₹200 extra to control the light and weather patterns' show outside (clouds and sunsets are free in-flight entertainment). Obviously, this doesn't mean you be a dick about it—if your co-passengers are inconvenienced, you don't tell them, 'Hey you plebian in the middle or aisle, kindly do not talk to the king of this row without a formal request to my courtiers, or give me a can of peanuts and off with their heads!'

A gentleman on the aisle on a flight to Dibrugarh obviously never got the memo. Across a three-hour flight, he would randomly lean across the middle, wake me up from my sleep and slap the window open or close as per his preference. And each time I would open the window, he wanted it shut, when I wanted it shut, he wanted to see the sun. He wanted exactly the opposite of what I wanted which obviously meant he worked with the government.

We got into an argument and I suddenly found myself surrounded by eight other people who were all his cronies scoffing, condescending and looking at me as if they were asking the air hostess for permission to murder me. Two rows of seats were just his cronies defending his honour to do whatever he pleased with the window or me. I briefly imagined what it would be like to fly outside the plane, seeing my own falling body plunge to the ground.

Upon landing, I discovered he was indeed a politician. Everything made sense. As I said: 25 per cent of all seats, occasionally for the Ravindra Gaikwad prototype.

Now, I'm not going to whinge about Air India. I have a few stories, but I'll avoid them because of the staff and crew of the airline, who recently have been making a sincere effort and deserve to be cut some slack.

Also, I still remember the man who stood up to Ravindra Gaikwad slapping him, which is nothing short of heroic. India's attitude towards Air India changes every few months. For the most part, we make the cliché jokes such as:

'Arrey, my grandmother is flight attendant, the pilot is her father and the plane was made by the same engineers as Pushpak, the food was made from the seats blessed by Jamshedji himself,' etc.

I know this because I've made similar jokes. And some of them are now invalid. I honestly don't care about the age of the air hostesses, as long as they do their job properly. And sometimes your age is advantageous. Occasionally, you'll fly an international flight with Indians who get wasted and behave oddly. On one such flight to Dubai, a gentleman was politely told by the air hostess, 'Beta, enough now. You've had three.' Can't argue with that. Guy stopped drinking and his face looked as if he wanted to ask the air hostess to sing him a lori (lullaby) to put him to bed.

And the Air India planes have gotten better, especially the

Dreamliner, which is genuinely spectacular. It's large, spacious and it doesn't have window shades—the windows change colour depending on the sun outside—that's some Feroz Khan sunglasses from the '70s level cool.

But, jokes on Air India are still valid with regards to delays, etc.,—so, it's all good. However, the jokes abate for a few weeks, every few months, in the time of crisis—whether it's airlifting Indians stuck in the Middle East or in Africa or Pakistanis and Indians stuck somewhere during COVID-19. Air India pilots and crew contracted coronavirus while attempting to rescue stranded people of all nations. You can't criticize that. That's heroism, again.

However, Air India is clearly mismanaged. There's a significantly high chance that if a private businessman was handling the airline across so many years, there may have been some criminal case against them—may have been. You never know. It's just unlikely that the government will investigate mismanagement of funds in their own backyard.

Buying Air India comes with a significant debt burden. The last time the government tried to sell the airline, it came with a debt burden of just a few thousand crores, i.e., ₹58,283 crore,[32] which on the basis of my (probably incorrect) calculations, could just about buy you about 10 RCBs.

That's right. You could use just the debt of Air India to start your own IPL league with 10 teams. Of course, no team would win if they follow the RCB model, but enough of that cliché joke.

---

[32] 'Air India sale: Debt burden on buyer to be ₹23,286 crore', *Business Today.in*, 27 January 2020, https://www.businesstoday.in/latest/corporate/story/air-india-sale-debt-burden-on-buyer-to-be-rs-23286-crore-243225-2020-01-27. Accessed on 9 February 2022.

Since shockingly no company decided to buy an airline with the debt of 10 IPL teams, the government decided to swallow two-third of the debt and bring down the debt to about ₹23,283 crore.[33] I wonder how the government magically swallowed that sizable debt, but they must be burping home loans, inflation and farting higher interest rates for weeks after.

Surprisingly, despite the debt reduction, there were still no takers.

How far does the government have to go to sell Air India? Swallow the full debt and give three private Dreamliners (for personal use) to every stakeholder who buys the airline? What?

The question remains: who would buy it?

The Tatas seem at the forefront and that would be a gharwapsi party for them—and by the time this book gets published, they may already have. It could also be the Ambanis, who are keen on buying anything that Adani has not bought.

But, as usual, I have a better idea…

## What I'll Do When I Become PM

We've been hovering around the answer in this piece itself. There is a business organization, which is not a business organization, but is a 'business' organization, but legally is not a business organization?—Board of Control for Cricket in India (BCCI). It calls itself the 'national governing body for cricket in India', which is even better than a business organization. The word 'govern' is in its brief. So, why not replace the government with *a* governing body?

---

[33]Ibid.

BCCI is already familiar with dealing in bureaucracy and 90 per cent of its head honchos are anyway India's top politicians—in transit, or otherwise. So, they know how to run through the red-tape and figure things out—despite what the court-appointed Committee of Administrators may have to say.

Here's some facts that once again may be off the mark.

In 2017, an average IPL team booked on average 35 tickets per flight and took a total of 10 flights, not including players and staff being flown in to the city, which is another five flights. That's a total of 15 flights, 35 tickets each. That's a total of 425 tickets per IPL team. There's eight IPL teams, bringing the total of just the number of flights during the IPL to 3,400 tickets.

This is not taking into account the TV crews, commentators, sponsors, politicians, investigative officers, Sharad Pawars, Mamata Banerjees, Amit Shah's son—which would easily increase this number ten-fold. You know, I'm not exaggerating.

Thus, the total number of flights booked for the IPL itself stands at 34,000 tickets! The value of those alone is about ₹20 crore, for one league. And I've not even started talking about the Indian men's, women's and other cricket teams, who are flying constantly. Plus, the same number of extra, including commentators, staff, etc. The total number of flights taken for cricket in India may stand at roughly ₹500 crore a year.

Additionally, the BCCI would sell sabudana vada, sabudana khichdi and sabudana protein bars (for the cricketers). All in all, owning an airline would save BCCI ₹250 crore per year. (Operational overheads at 50 per cent).

Now, you'd say, 'Sorabh, congrats that you have a calculator on your laptop, but that still pales in comparison to the amount of debt and value of Air India.'

Ah, yes. But, you forget that I'm a cricket fan and while crunching numbers gives us orgasms, outthinking the batsman makes us even more excited.

The BCCI also has a history of sponsorships. Ask Star Sports that spent ₹16,348 crore to buy IPL rights for five years.[34] And, that's just for one tournament. Can you imagine the sponsorship they would get for an airline?

Yes, everything on BCCI's Air India will be sponsored: 'Welcome to DFL presents Bangalore to Jaipur, Ma'am. Please put on your safety belts brought to you by Vivo Mobile and fasten it using your Vodafone buckle. In the case of an emergency brought to you by American Express, a float sponsored by Mahesh Tutorials will rescue you and take you straight to see India vs South Africa tri-series in Zimbabwe! Over to you, Harsha for the air report outside...'

'Harsha, here. On the wing of the plane, with this gorgeous logo of Rupa Frontline. As we ready for take-off, the wind sponsored by Indigo Airlines looks good and it should help the pilots though some turbulence is expected...whoosh, I'm dead...' etc.

I've solved yet another conundrum. Kindly make me head of BCCI already. Sorry, Sourav. This time Sorabh wins.

I will be happy to be aviation minister also. Though, of course, I'm aiming to be PM.

---

[34]PTI, 'Star India buys IPL media rights for record Rs 16,347 crore. What do the figures mean?', *The New Indian Express*, 4 September 2017, https://www.newindianexpress.com/sport/cricket/2017/sep/04/star-india-buys-ipl-media-rights-for-record-rs-16347-crore-what-do-the-figures-mean-1652398--1.html. Accessed on 16 February 2022.

P.S.: Tatas bought out Air India, which is a far better idea than my suggestion. It's also a fascinating tale—I always enjoyed the story of JRD Tata. India didn't have an airline, India didn't have a licensed pilot. He decided, 'I'll become both.' And now Tata has Air India back. Quite historic.

# 9

# *Income Tax: Note of Thanks*

Both my parents used to work for the Income Tax. So, serving the nation has been in our blood. Additionally, my surname is 'Pant', which may lead you to imply that my lineage involves garments, but it apparently does not. And, I am still not sure if this is true, but maybe it is, so here it goes: Pant, pronounced P-u-n-t-t, is actually the Marathi word for minister. That's because many of my forefathers used to be ministers in the courts of Maratha kings. So, once again: serving the nation is literally in my blood. Apparently. I am still not sure if this is real.

Now all this is based on what my relatives tell me and my surname could mean something completely different, but whatever makes me sound more impressive without having achieved anything impressive is probably okay. It must also be worth mentioning that I am not a Maharashtrian. I wish I was—Maratha people have a history of hard work and have fire within and I wish I had those qualities. But, I personally don't. I'm from Uttarakhand (the original UK) and we Pants are all over the world. I was surprised to find us settled in the US, Europe, Nepal and Bhutan as well which just opens it out to free housing while travelling.

Anyway, history of the Pants aside, I have a history of

serving the nation.

In my current avatar as a Pant, I have served India by paying an enormous amount of tax. And some of you think that makes me sound like an elitist and you're imagining me taking my private helicopter (diesel as fuel) to buy groceries, while shouting at poor people (identified as anyone who is not me) with insults such as:

'Yo, gareebs. You so gareeb, you probably have to peel your own bananas.' (I have a personal banana peeler.)

'Yo, gareebs. Do you even pay tax surcharge? Loser!' (I paid tax surcharge, until 2020.)

'Yo, gareebs. Why do you walk? What a loser.' (I get carried around on the backs of members of FICCI and the Chambers of Commerce.)

That's far from the truth. I don't think my earning capacity defines who I am as a person. I acknowledge that there are people who work ridiculously harder than me for far less money and I'm truly lucky and privileged to have the opportunities I have. I suck as a person and an earner and I acknowledge the same.

But...

Here's what some people tell you about taxation in India—it is high. It is so high that it should be illegal to do it anywhere except in Amsterdam and certain states in America and Canada.

If you're earning above ₹1 crore (not me—this is for my friend Sorabh Putin), then here's roughly what you're paying in taxes:

- 25 per cent of income (post expenses),
- 10 per cent surcharge,

- 10 per cent TDS,
- 12–18 per cent GST (you don't even realize when you're paying this),
- 35 per cent indirect taxes (average tax on any consumer goods is around 25 per cent, on fuel it's 70 per cent, on flights it's 50 per cent, even your EMI has a tax component etc.)

Now, obviously I'm not a financial expert or a chartered accountant, which is proven by the fact that the above calculation brings taxes to 117–123 per cent of your income, which seems essentially impossible—you can't pay more tax than you earn, even though we are close. And while all this is exaggeration, actual resources say that total taxation in India (if you're paying income tax) is about 55–60 per cent!

Again, since I'm not an editor for a financial newspaper, these figures may not be entirely accurate, but I'm pretty sure they will be. Because I have a calculator. And my forefathers were ministers.

Minister+calculator=verified facts

The amount of tax that sneaks up on you is absolutely ridiculous. Let's take fuel as an example. India has the highest tax on fuel in the world! In my last research, the amount was 69 per cent. Sixty-nine per cent because the government is turning you around and 69ing you, with tax. So each time any government announces a reduction on fuel prices, I'm not impressed. I'd love to hear them announce a reduction in taxation. If you run an airline in India, congrats. You're immediately paying 16–50 per cent more than the average global rates for aviation fuel.[35] It's possible our aviation fuel

---

[35] 'Aviation fuel price 50% higher in India', *Business Standard*, 23 January 2013,

comes infused with Red Bull or some special boost (maybe actual Boost is the secret of the plane's energy?) or it could be that it's stupidly high.

It goes without saying that Jet Airways may have stayed afloat if their operational expenses were 10 per cent less, but since I'm not Naresh Goyal's spokesperson (yet), I say 'no comment' (for now).

Barely 3 per cent of India pays income tax (source: income tax uncle I met at my parent's party. He assured me this figure was correct and then proceeded to spend 12 minutes telling me to use onion oil to regrow my hair). This is not unusual—apparently, even developed countries have barely 8–10 per cent people paying income tax. This is because agriculture is mostly exempt and so are children, homemakers, the retired, etc., etc.

But, 2.5 per cent of the country pays income tax (source: Economic Times. Uncle was off by barely 0.5 per cent), of this number 4 per cent pay 60 per cent of the total income tax collected.[36] If you have money to buy this book, there's a high chance you're one of those Indians.

The government won't, so I would like to personally thank you for helping build this nation.

And that's what I would like from the government. A personal thanks.

I'm not complaining (actually I am) about the taxes in India being so ridiculously high. It makes me jealous of those

---

https://www.business-standard.com/article/economy-policy/aviation-fuel-price-50-higher-in-india-111111700039_1.html. Accessed on 4 March 2022.

[36]'Budget 2020: The deceptive rise in India's income tax base', *The Economic Times*, 2 February 2020, https://economictimes.indiatimes.com/wealth/tax/budget-2020-the-deceptive-rise-in-indias-income-tax-base/articleshow/73868046.cms?from=mdr. Accessed on 16 February 2022.

who don't pay taxes and use bribery and black money to evade taxation. I'm constantly impressed by them as to how they avoided the tax net.

The Panama Papers or housing scams or Swiss banks or flying to London—one part of me is furious and another part is so impressed by them, thinking how they got away. I would neither have the interest, nor the inclination, and specifically not even the methods and definitely not the income to do the same.

What I do know is that paying 55 per cent tax is nuts.

If you want context—taxation of 55 per cent is comparable to 'rich' European countries, most of which offer either free education and/or transport and/or food and impeccable infrastructure.

Unlike...

Obviously India is a little bigger than most European countries. In fact, India's population is almost double of the whole of Europe. One country is double the people of an entire continent! Technically, India has more population than all, but one continent—and that continent happens to be the one where India exists. How are we not a continent ourselves? Or a planet. Forget Pluto, I demand that India be designated as a dwarf planet—at least that way when China tries to claim our land, it's not only an international, but a universal crime.

Our population is ridiculous and we have many people in abject poverty struggling to make ends meet (I still don't know what that term means, 'make ends meet', it sounds like twerking) and it is only logical that the ones who have the means must help uplift those who do not. That's the only way a society can function. And your historic privilege and its benefits should come with your responsibility to help others. I completely understand what a great person I am for paying my taxes.

I've been paying taxes since I was 18 because that's when I started working. My parents were with the income tax department, so you'd think that came with some family benefits, but no. My mom once told me, 'Please pay all appropriate taxes and more. What will the department say if we don't?' It was such an annoying attitude. Honestly, why did my parents even sit for the UPSC exams and become civil servants if they didn't learn how to game the system? This kind of honesty is not what built tycoons.

Paying taxes should not come with an award system, I don't want a Nobel Prize or a Red and White Bravery Award. But, I do think I deserve some kind of mention.

## What I'll Do When I Become PM

I will personally thank each and every one of the million people that have paid those high number of taxes. Each time I make a speech, I will end it by mentioning some of them:

> '...and that's why India should be a dwarf planet. Now, I'd like to thank some people for their contributions to my YouTube page. They contributed by paying income tax. Richvender Singh, Fatima Dollar, Ameer Tripathi, Gulabuddin Chequewalla, Richa Rich, all the names in the Panama Papers and of course Sorabh Pant, i.e. myself. If you'd like to contribute and be named personally in my next speech, click the link below (incometaxindiaefiling.gov.in) and maybe I'll say your

name next time! Subscribe, share and like my videos so I can beat Donald Trump's YouTube page. Thanks.'

Each video may last for a few hours, but you can't tell me that won't be about as entertaining as the proceedings of the Parliament anyway.

## small thoughts

*The Parliament has the potential to be considerably more entertaining than it is at the moment. Every few weeks a speech from the Parliament does go viral, but there is no consistency in this. As Instagram reels have taught us—consistency is key, quality be damned.*

*Our politicians need to embrace modern developments to stay trending. Creating Instagram reels in the middle of delivering a speech at the Parliament is the way to go.*

*Want to make a point about petrol prices?*

*Use an Instagram filter with Vin Diesel's face to make the obvious pun, 'Diesel ka bhav badh gaya hai—Vin Diesel? Haan, French mein 'Vin' matlab 'wine' aur agar meri van mein vin dalta toh aur sasta padhta [The price of diesel has risen—Vin Diesel? In French, Vin means wine and if my van worked on wine, that would be cheaper].'*

*Want to stage a walkout in the Parliament?*

*Don't forget to do it while playing classic songs in the background as you do—'Chalte Chalte' from 1976 or 2003, Vanessa Carlton's 'A Thousand Miles', 1997's 'Daud' if you're more eclectic or even Foo Fighters' 'Walk' if you're into that.*

*Don't like a Bill being passed?*

*Like every Indian newspaper or Amul hoarding copywriter, use the fact that the word 'bill' rhymes with the word 'dil' (heart) and use the trillions of dialogues from Indian films involving the word and mix it up.* Bill Chahta Hai *(What the bill wants),* Yeh Bill Deewana *(This bill is crazy),* Bill to Pagal Hai *(This bill is mad) or even do a tribute to* Kill Bill *but without the samurais and death.*

*Basically puns and Instagram—that's my solution for making the Parliament relevant again. Do send me my cheque for consulting in my next income tax rebate.*

# 10

## *Buying the News*

An entertainment supplement of a popular Indian newspaper mentions in certain articles that they are 'advertorials' and not news articles. I appreciate that—the honesty and acceptance that some things in the supplement is an advertisement and some journalists are copywriters working for an advertising agency that publishes daily.

I enjoy most of the entertainment supplements across newspapers. It's a great way to analyse which celebrities are making money. If you can afford to be on the front page, you're probably doing superbly. If like me, you can only afford to be on the eighth page under 'Miscellaneous Entertainment', you're okay. Reading these supplements is a subtle way of reading a Forbes list of the rich in entertainment industry.

Everyone in the front page has a wealth manager. Or two. Unless the front page is about death or an issue like sexism or racism or theft—then we aren't sure if they have a wealth manager, and it would be worth reading their will to figure that out.

Every newspaper in India does it—it's not a big deal. We're all bought by something or the other. Either by our ideals, our politics, our religion, our morality or simply by actual money.

And money is the best way to buy more things.

What I enjoy about entertainment newspapers is the honesty. They're telling you, 'Hey, you want to be here? Either be really worthy of the news, say something controversial, have something controversial happen to you, give birth, die or just pay us. It's all good. We don't judge. This is an advertorial; this is the news.' It explains why you will see stories in these newspapers carrying headlines like:

'Sonakshi Sinha is afraid of lifts'
'Varun Dhawan ate cake—Bollywood congratulates him'
'Ajay Devgn changes his name to Ajay Likesguns'
'Priyanka Chopra is a person'
'Shahid Kapoor has a laptop'
'Kanika Kapoor comments on Kanika Kapoor controversy'

It's good. I appreciate it. I wish this kind of honesty was found across all newspapers and news media. While Bollywood may think it has money to buy advertorials, political parties and the governments have money to place 'ads' in news channels, or the media in general. It's done in subtle and smart ways, but you know it's happening. These ads could also be news stories—I'm not saying they are and I'm not saying they are not.

My mother had a theory about a particular newspaper (let's not name it) which was this: 'You can tell which party is going to win the election depending on how X newspaper reports them. You can also tell which politician is losing favour by how they report on them. I read X newspaper because it's basically a daily exit poll for elections that may or may not happen.' News channels in India are so abundantly upfront about their political leanings that the joy of watching them is gone. I would watch these channels to see through the bullshit and figure out which direction they leaned on, but now even that game is invalid.

Without naming channels, you can see it. Let's say there are three trending stories in a day:

- 'Electric autorickshaws in Delhi will now be coloured black and purple.'
- 'Random actress says she will not delete TikTok app.'
- 'Central government increases the price of petrol.'

News Channel 1: 'Kejriwal has lost it. Delhi is losing faith in Kejriwal. Purple autorickshaws—how will people differentiate between the mode of transport and brinjal? Delhi barely has electricity—where will autos get electricity? Has Kejriwal ruined Delhi again? Is he a brinjal?'

News Channel 2: 'We will now do a 12-hour debate on whether Random Actress should be officially designated a citizen of China, Pakistan, Hong Kong and also why these leftist liberal sickulars hate Modiji and will not stand with him.'

News Channel 3: 'Great news for India. We will collect more tax money because of the increase in petrol price. Hopefully, this great initiative will help collect money to make autorickshaws in every state except Delhi run on electricity.'

News Channel 4: 'Kejriwal helps reduce pollution in Delhi. Modiji has ruined us again. Now let's see this video that proves that pandas are aliens from Mars…' etc.

It's pretty blatant and annoying because I can't use my intelligence to guess who is bought. And this is not specific to India—every country in the world now has news channels that are peddling party propaganda in the guise of reporting news. And it's convenient to say they are 'bought', as if there is a direct connection between the political party and the news channel—which there is not.

The connection is indirect. The news channel or outlet is a small company owned by some big company one of whose other bigger companies are owned/financed by another company that is owned by the cousin of the aunt of a mainstream politician, who happens to be from the party in power—either in state or in the Centre.

Probably diktats come in from the editorial board telling journalists, 'Friends, if you'd like to continue getting your salaries, kindly avoid doing any stories disparaging Mr Mutual Fund and the party he comes from, okay? If you'd like to continue doing those stories, don't worry, I'm sure you can start a news company online that is financed by radical college students and move to the suburbs of lower Noida.' And everyone complies. Because for most of us truth is negotiable, comfort is not. I don't blame anyone for complying. Everyone has their needs and responsibilities—just don't scream at me about journalistic standards when you're so obviously following none of them.

There has been more than one instance where a political party has approached us to perform for their anniversary celebration and on one occasion for a tweet praising someone—and so far I've said no.

So far.

Sorry, Cobrapost.

However, I don't necessarily blame the celebrities that were bought by politics. Political parties are corporations— how is this different from endorsing a drink or a car or a mobile phone? Is it because we assume that the celebrity has 'sold' their ideology, given up their moral compass in exchange for cash?

Yes, it is a big deal that you've sold your morals for money. But, what if your morals were anyway in that direction and now they're giving you money to endorse those morals?

That's fine, right?

Some of the celebrities named in the Cobrapost expose still merrily promote certain politics and no one cares. We do not care. Our media is bought—so, why does it matter if our individuals are also bought?

Imagine your career is not going as well as you imagined it would. Whatever you did—acting, comedy, cricket, singing, whatever—is all over now. But, your bills have not stopped. Your EMI remains, your kids have to go to college, you have to plan that trip abroad or you're just plain greedy.

And a political party approaches you for endorsing them for money. They do the same for spokespersons. So, why not you? You anyway agree with them—and now they're paying you. Cool. Might as well agree.

The big advantage for so many celebrities is the publicity. They're cognizant of this. Look at the number of former film folk that are now blatantly endorsing politics—they get the spotlight, they get the attention—for suddenly having political insights that are spoon-fed to them. It helps rekindle the career. It adds more drama to life.

And that explains the (some) news channels as well. The implication is that news channels and papers are 'bought'. There's a high chance that they're just (indirectly) getting paid to endorse what they already believe. They're getting attention. And attention implies advertisers and who doesn't love advertisers?

You sell controversy and one-sided views, people watch them, your TRPs rise and advertisers come in. There's this anecdote (I'm pretty sure it's true—but maybe it's not) about India TV and Rajat Sharma. When India TV started, it was trying to focus on actual journalism: uncovering scams, unearthing real stories. The views were close to nothing. Rajat Sharma realized that they need to stir things up—and then started the India TV legend of ridiculous stories (note: these below may be a mix of actual stories and nonsense stories from my mind):

'Was this lady a snake in previous birth?'

'Your husband may be an alien.'

'Is this alien a snake lady who is your mother?'

'Is Joseph Goebbels still alive and CEO of his own company in Vietnam? Photos...'

'Has this Guru been to the afterlife? Here's video proof...'

The move worked and India TV's views went through the roof. People were suddenly watching and that's when India TV would throw them a story about scams and real news. One half of all programming would be utter stupidity and the other half would be journalism.

At least, that was the intention. I'm not sure that's the case for the channel or news channels in general or even for the news channel I named, I don't know. At least that 'half and half' was done out of 'innovation' and induced by demand and to get advertisers. Now, news channels seem to be told what to do, what to say and how to say it. The advertisers are the political parties and once again they are dictating the news.

The 'half and half' is gone—now, it's just full.

Everything now has to sound dramatic on news channels— they are not selling you news, but entertainment with political views in the background because you can't fill up 24 hours of a news cycle with balanced opinions. Who would watch that? Even balanced people want to watch imbalanced people so that they can feel more balanced in comparison.

## What I'll Do When I Become PM

Every news channel will be labelled 'advertorial'. Each news report has to begin with an ad for the political party that's indirectly 'running' the channel. They can continue advertising with other advertisers—no problems there. But, they should let us know who is 'running' them.

Additionally, there would be no more 24-hour news channels, except in the case of an emergency or an attack, and every news channel in India can only run for four hours a day. The rest of the 20 hours, they just have to show footage of Indians of all religions, political backgrounds, castes, creeds talking to each other. That's it. They won't have to go far to get the footage. Such footage exists literally everywhere in India. If you're causing communal discord and disharmony of any kind, you should show the other side as well.

Show footage from a tea stall, an office, a cricket training camp, a film studio. Show such footage to show the real India, if you're also showing the worst of India.

P.S.: While this seems like an attack on conservative news channels, it also applies to those news channels both online and offline that believe that all conservatives are bigoted idiots—all the ultra-woke super liberal portals that seem to have this moral standing which refuses to even attempt to comprehend people with differing views. Let's not pretend that if you were in power, things would be significantly different. They may be, but I doubt it.

All of you radicals on all sides can equally go f.o.

## small thoughts

*Fake news and false agendas being spread on WhatsApp, etc., is a big problem. But, you can fight this menace—on a regular basis, just start spreading rumours that harm no one. You can start with the one below.*

*For example, if you want to establish that former child actor, Jugal Hansraj, is actually South African, then all you need is a believable back story and some facts—fake or real, who cares? This is all lies anyway.*

*WhatsApp Forward/YT Video:*

*Jugal Hansraj is a South African national. It all started when he was shooting for Shekhar Kapur's Masoom as a child. Naseeruddin Shah had just returned from a shoot in South Africa and happened to have a few feathers of jackass penguins with him. He gave four each to each of the child actors and told them to keep it to remember him. When Jugal grew up and started shaving, his shaving brush was lost and he urgently needed to shave for a meeting. Finding the feathers from Naseeruddin Shah, he thought why not? Jugal (doing Jugad) used the same for shaving and went for the meeting. The meeting was amazing. Jugal got $2 million from a subsidiary of Google called Southern Animatronics or S.A. Jugal began to wonder if this was all connected. He decided to go to South Africa, where he was summoned by Nelson Mandela! Mr Mandela told him he loved Masoom and Jugal was very cute in the movie and his daughter was a member of 'The Hansrajes', a Jugal Hansraj fan club. Jugal was amazed, he had no fan clubs in India—this was fate. He wept openly in front of Mr Mandela and asked if he could become a South African national. He now trains actors in Johannesburg and works as a Jackass Penguin Conservationist by day.*

*Spread the harmless lies, enjoy.*

# 11

# WhatsApp vs News: Lies

Many people are happy to rely on WhatsApp to believe lies they want to believe because confirmation bias is a joyful thing. In case you don't know what confirmation bias is, it basically means that you believe whatever information you want to believe as long as it agrees with your world view: which explains religion and the banking system.

This is why people will forward stuff that they think is true because it conveniently aligns with what they believe—and nothing works better than the fake forwards on WhatsApp during COVID-19. These included things like:

## Imran Khan is in hospital because he tried to drink camel urine

I'm not sure who this was trolling exactly: people who suggested *gaumutra* (cow urine) is the cure or the PM of Pakistan or camels or just Photoshop. Honestly, it would be hilarious if it were true because unlike cows—who I love and must be mentioned—camels don't exactly seem as laid-back if you attempt to drink their urine. Camels don't seem like they'd give up their bodily fluids without a fight, even if they can store more fluids for the desert. Despite that some people in the Middle East consume camel urine, which reminds me that water is my favourite drink.

## 'There's a Chinese TV show called 'My Secret Terrius' that talks of coronavirus in 2018—was COVID-19 all a Chinese conspiracy?' (Even though the show in question was South Korean.)

I will not comment on the last sentence because I want to do shows in Beijing and Macau once this blows over, but let me clarify that, in case you didn't know, coronavirus is a group of viruses. It was first discovered in the 1960s—but everyone was distracted because Beatlemania is bigger than viruses. I'd give anything to be infected by Sgt. Peppers right now; I prefer them as a group to coronavirus—that group of tiny little bastards—that cause a disease. Coronaviruses cause diseases that include MERS, SARS (appeared in China in 2002) and COVID-19 as well as others.

It's not beyond the realms of possibility that a corny South Korean TV show would use it as a plot device much like Crime Patrol may use a computer hacker as a plot point for a murder. It doesn't imply that Anonymous is a conspiracy by India.

## Asterix Gets Involved

Much like China, France had also gotten involved. In 2017, Asterix fought a villain called Coronavirus in *Asterix and the Chariot Race*. I love Asterix and I assume he defeated the villainous Coronavirus using some magic potion (vaccine?) Yet no one accused France of having information of the virus like they did with China—which is a bit weird. It leads me to give a suggestion to French scientists working on a COVID vaccine to ensure they at least name it 'Getafix's magic potion' or at the very least 'Vitalstatistix'.

It would be an easy one to write on a vial: consume 2 grams of Vitalstatistix and your body's vital statistics shall hurriedly improve. It's a pun that both Goscinny and Uderzo have awaited since they began fighting Romans, in their head.

## Every building is infected, especially the one next to you

I don't know who these people are that start rumours like, 'Confirmed by Medical Police of India Fraternity that Laxmikant–Pyarelal Building Complex is infected by COVID-19, which has mutated turning the whole building into rabid cocker spaniels.' What joy do these people get? How bored are you sitting at home during the lockdown that you think, 'You know what I always hated that Jagdeesh Mishra from that Laxmikant building over there. He took ₹200 from me for a taxi in 2008 and still hasn't paid me back. What badla, what revenge can I have... Idea!' BROADCAST TO ALL.

My favourite part is when they 'verify' the rumours by claiming that it was from someone official—I have a doctor friend, confirmed personally by UNESCO, WHO has said this, Dr Pepper from University of Mississauga, Patanjalee CEO, the President of Bolivia herself—and people are stupid enough to believe it just because it has been typed.

## Russia has killed 100 people that had COVID-19

You want to believe this because it aligns with your theory of KGB and subterfuge and thinking that 2020 is Stalin's year. It's obviously not true. Isn't it? Is it? This one we will never know.

## Prince Charles has coronavirus

This is obviously a rumour and never happened.

## Boris Johnson has coronavirus

Absolutely ridiculous—people will say just about anything. I mean just because you disagreed with him on England exiting Brexit does not mean you want viruses to enter his body. Have some empathy. Next you'll tell me that Tom Hanks, Shahid Afridi, Idris Elba, Pink, Patrick Ewing, Kanika Kapoor, Tormund from *Game of Thrones* are all infected.

## Take a deep breath and if you can hold your breath for 10 seconds without coughing, it means you have no infection

Or it means that you know how to count till 10. Which means you probably also know how to understand when WhatsApp can be bullshit.

## China is shooting COVID-19 patients

A badly edited video was doing the rounds where three Chinese 'doctors' with guns walk outside a van and there's gun shots and squeals. It seemed pretty clear that the video was three separate videos combined into one and not like *Lord of the Rings*, more like *Sacred Games*, *Mirzapur* and *Kung Fu Hustle* presented as a trilogy, which honestly sounds like a great trilogy.

The Chinese clarified this video by saying those were not doctors, but policemen in protective COVID-19 medical gear who shot rabid dogs, which is an explanation that leaves more questions than answers. This is much like another video where a woman was dragged out of her car by four policemen as she screamed; she was pinned on the floor like a pig after which she fainted.[37] The rumour went that the woman was shot because she had COVID-19. The truth is that a city had banned private cars during the crisis and this lady had defied the curfew.

## Helicopters will disinfect the city of Mumbai

Our cook told us this (she had stopped coming after the lockdown—relax): 'Modiji is going to send out a fleet of helicopters to disinfect the city from the top.' The rumour may have started because China (again) apparently did a similar thing with trucks in Hubei province and if you're spreading a rumour, it should at least make India look cooler than China. It's a different thing that we don't have those many helicopters lying around (unless Mr Ambani lends his, which he might). So, I'm surprised no one spread this rumour: 'Modiji himself

---

[37] Kundu, Chayan. 'Fact Check: Did police publicly kill coronavirus-infected woman in China?', India Today, 10 February 2020, https://www.indiatoday.in/fact-check/story/fact-check-did-police-publicly-kill-coronavirus-infected-woman-in-china-1645123-2020-02-10. Accessed on 2 March 2022.

will pilot a fleet of Russian military planes that will not only rid Mumbai of COVID-19, but also stop crime and induce time travel so we can go ahead to a time where India never faced COVID-19.'

I understand the psychology behind this: these rumours are just people's way of dealing; spreading this unverified nonsense makes them think they are doing something, even if what they're doing is mostly spreading chaos. #GoogleIt should be a mandatory hashtag before you can forward any WhatsApp news forward. A lot of people think you have to climb a mountain to access Google—just #GoogleIt, it takes 20 seconds.

The governments across India instead decided to pass laws to prevent rumours from spreading on WhatsApp. You could have faced a year in jail (or a fine) under Section 54 of the National Disaster Management Act for spreading false news on WhatsApp.

An FIR was registered against a Twitter user in Hyderabad by the Cyberabad Police.[38] @theskindoctor13 had circulated an obviously satirical/fake news article which said, 'Cyberabad Police bans the sale of oranges in the city [because the] saffron color of oranges is hurting the sentiments of Muslims.' It was satirical as it was clearly mentioned in the 'news' article that it was satire.

Obviously, this was a joke. Even the most fundamental Muslim will not see this article and think, 'Finally! How dare they sell saffron coloured oranges? I'd also like papayas,

---

[38] '#WeStandWithSkinDoctor trends after Cyberabad police register FIR against Retd Major Neelam Singh over 'satirical' post', *The Free Press Journal*, 28 April 2020, https://www.freepressjournal.in/viral/westandwithskindoctor-trends-after-cyberabad-police-register-fir-against-retd-major-neelam-singh-over-satirical-post. Accessed on 9 February 2022.

training tennis balls, saffron powder, mangoes, traffic cones and carrots to be banned.' It's a dumb joke and any discernible person would understand that. While communal harmony can be 'disrupted' in India at the drop of a hat ('Our religion does not have hats, how dare you? This is blasphemy'), there must be a limit to what constitutes causing this disharmony.

Someone said that from the Cyberabad Police's point of view it made sense to file an FIR just to protect the fact that they did not pass any such rule. I'm not sure what to make of that, but a statement saying they did not do so would probably have communicated the same? No?

We've had multiple cases of Indians being jailed or worse for spreading 'false' news or jokes. Arguably, the most prominent example would be Professor Ambikesh Mahapatra who was arrested in 2012 for forwarding cartoons about Mamata Banerjee.[39] The list of civilians arrested or threatened or worse for spreading 'rumours' or jokes is long and spreads from Maharashtra to UP to Bihar to every state. You know what worse implies, so I will not get into it.

But, let's focus purely on the legal action taken against civilians. Anyone spreading malicious rumours should probably be held accountable, ideally with a warning and arguably further for repeat offenses. The problem being what is considered 'malicious' in India—the term is so loose that malice when not intended can be found and where intended could be lost, depending on who is filing the case and also where elections will occur. But, even that guideline should

---

[39]Banerjie, Monideepa. 'Professor Jailed For Circulating Mamata Cartoons to be Compensated, Says Court', NDTV, 10 March 2015, https://www.ndtv.com/india-news/double-the-compensation-of-jadavpur-professor-arrested-for-circulating-mamata-cartoons-court-tells-g-745593. Accessed on 10 February 2022.

apply equally to civilians, politicians and journalists. Many people assume that journalists are typically held accountable for their statements ONLY when they do not support the government in power. Otherwise they have a free handle to do and say pretty much whatever they want.

Now, let's talk about news channels and journalists. I'm going to be as vague as possible because my legal department is my brother in-law's sister who is into corporate law and I doubt any news channel will file a suit against me for copyright infringement or something.

A few years back, a prominent news channel in India was accused of doctoring videos which led to violence toward certain people. Please understand: a news channel edited and doctored videos and aired it as real news, repeatedly. It put the lives of people at risk and this was done intentionally. Apparently, the channel suffered 'grave' consequences and received a warning and was fined ₹50,000.

In another story: a news channel covered a particular attack so closely that they gave away strategic information to the terrorists, who may have used this information to their advantage. The result was a one-day ban that was later repealed.

The sheer number of falsehoods perpetuated on a daily basis by news channels in India is ridiculous. I'm not going to talk about the truly hateful and communal coverage, but the purely foolish.

Indian-American scientist Shawna Pandya was confirmed to have been shortlisted for NASA's 2018 space mission.[40]

---

[40]PTI, 'Shawna Pandya To Become Third Indian-Origin Woman To Fly In Space', NDTV, 10 February 2017, https://www.ndtv.com/indians-abroad/indian-origin-woman-neurosurgeon-picked-for-nasa-space-mission-1657881. Accessed on 21 February 2022.

Indian news channels decided to take a leap of faith on this story and went ahead and announced that Shawna would be flying to Mars, becoming a Martian, colonizing Jupiter, becoming a meteoroid and crossing over to the Kuiper belt. Shawna had to come out and say that no such thing happened. But, Indian news channels had already confirmed the same—so, she couldn't deny it.

'Dawood Ibrahim has coronavirus.' This was great news because at least coronavirus caught Dawood, the hope being that COVID-19 at least would not let Dawood escape on bail. News channels celebrated this news and made the standard platitudes about karma, etc. Dawood's brother rubbished the claims. Of course, in this particular case, I trust Indian news over Dawood or his brother.

About two weeks into the lockdown in India, another news channel put out a news story that the government had started trains for migrant labourers. The story spread like wildfire across WhatsApp and approximately 1,500 migrant labourers showed up at Bandra Station, looking for some escape to get back to their homes at a point when all roads to their homes seemed blocked. This happened at a crucial juncture of trying to control the virus.

What happened to the channel? Oh, absolutely nothing. In fact, the channel, who is fan of the central government, criticized the state government (different party) for not being able to control the crowds who had showed up on the basis of rumours the news channel had spread in the first place!

Imagine robbing a bank and then blaming the police for allowing banks to be robbed—that describes some Indian news channels perfectly.

There's been multiple politicians and news channels,

especially during COVID-19 times that have used the virus as an excuse to spout hate towards a community, a religion or just each other. They have prompted unrest, confusion, hatred and had a sum total of (probably) zero FIRs filed against.

We hold civilians, bloggers, social media users, perfomers, actors and comedians (notice how I shoved us in there) to have higher journalistic standards than journalists. This makes me feel good and bad about myself.

## What I'll Do When I Become PM

If a news channel spreads fake news, then they would be punished with false rumours being spread about them on WhatsApp for one week. The people who believe them are anyway the kind of people who believe their news—so, it may reach a point where the news channel or the newsperson believes it themselves.

Some suggestions for the rumours:

- 'Journalist Pankaj Godbole has died.'
- 'Pankaj Godbole is alive.'
- 'Pankaj Godbole is a zombie and it's rumoured by doctors from the University of Philippines in New York that listening to Mr Godbole can cause you to also become a zombie. This is a special medical condition that spreads from aural (ear canal) cavities in the body. Additionally, Dr James Jameson from WHO in the South China Sea has done three years of study in 12 days to find out that even looking at Mr Godbole may cause you to turn into a zombie. The spread is caused by visual (eyes) cavities in the

body. Doctors have warned that listening or seeing Mr Godbole can infect you. This zombie disease may cause you to die, live again, walk around like a zombie, eat your underarm hair, eat plants, try and eat your family members, drink water from under the sink, hallucinate about lies and, worse, lead you to believe things that are not true.'

- 'Pankaj Godbole is a vada pav. Anthony Bourdain had once said that Mr Godbole is the tastiest vada pav outside the Mississippi and he must be eaten. If you see Mr Godbole please throw some chutney on him and bite him.'

Feel free to insert your own suggestions in your mind.

## small thoughts

*A lady in my building was always rude to domestic workers. However, she was ridiculously polite to the rest of us, which led us to believe that she had some problems. I'd have more patience for someone who was rude to everyone irrespective of their financial or perceived social status.*

*This was before the pandemic.*

*Once the pandemic hit, the same lady's domestic worker left her (presumably they were waiting for an excuse) and she completely changed her tune. Left with no one to help her in the house, she was sugary sweet and nice to all the domestic workers left in the building, begging someone to get her some help. It was hilarious, this sudden change in her. And she was not alone.*

*If this pandemic did one thing, it was to remind millions of Indians about the importance of all the people working hard in their homes, and to treat them like human beings instead of some kind of robotic humanoids created as a vessel to receive their abuse.*

*People that would scream at cooks for using the wrong lift in a building were suddenly begging the same cooks to find another cook to cook for them, 'Didi, come on, I think of you as my friend, my confidante, let's go for shopping and wear matching outfits. I'd like to get a locket made in gold with your face on it. Just please, I beg you—find me a cook.' Maybe one of humanity's greatest challenges was the trigger for people to treat other people as humans. Not a bad upside.*

# 12

## (An Outdated Chapter) on Nepotism in Bollywood

*This piece was originally written before the death of the terrific actor Sushant Singh Rajput. I've decided not to add that dimension to this piece because to unpack all that happened would make this more emotional than funny. And also because his news vis-à-vis nepotism in Bollywood has been covered by enough journalists and comedians (anchors) in news debates.*

*I honestly don't even agree with a lot of what I've written in this chapter now. But, it's an interesting experiment to read and proves how quickly opinions can change. I would have changed them in this chapter itself, but I'm too lazy.*

While the cliques and gangs and the family clubs of Bollywood are often accused of *being* cliques and gangs and family clubs of Bollywood that make it hard for outsiders to enter, things are changing and have been for quite some time.

The change has been gradual and also been an upside of OTT platforms like Netflix, Amazon Prime, Hotstar, Voot, ALTBalaji, YouTube, Twitch, Xvideos, Porndub, Cricinfo, Vimeo, TikTok, Takatak, tok tik, tock tock, mitron and about

12,000 others. They promote what people want to watch, not what Bollywood wants to give. This explains why Indian TV shows (at least on OTTs) are suddenly grittier, more real and significantly more engrossing than 90 per cent of Bollywood films.

The basis for my study is an in-depth survey I did with involving my family, friends, myself and social media platforms. The survey was done using this high-end technology called 'talking', so there's a chance this is not a defining survey on the issue, but it seems close.

As per this ISO-9001 uncertified survey, over the last two years, the biggest Indian web series (*Scam 1992, Aspirants, Paatal Lok, Mirzapur, Family Man* and *Sacred Games*) have been way better than Bollywood's biggest (attempted) blockbusters (*Sardar Ka Grandson, Radhe, The Girl on the Train, Saina, Laxmii, The Big Bull*) which are watched ironically for the purpose of meme culture.

It's also telling that most of those web series featured actors and directors from non-film families whereas most of the films feature Bollywood's own family (wo)men.

Conclusion from this survey: Bollywood sucks and nepotism has ruined the industry?

And that may not be true. In fact, if I would be so bold as to say it's wrong, Bollywood does not suck even though it is often... sucky. Yes, I used the word 'sucky' in a book which is not about a teenage vampire girl in the '90s.

Over the last decade, the industry has had a good mix of nonsensical masala films as well as good movies that tell real stories. And as a connoisseur of the arts (self-titled, check my Twitter bio), I enjoy both.

I'm happy to see Akshay Kumar pretend to rescue an entire

cricket team of hostages from terrorists with one dialogue as I am to watch Ayushmann Khurrana play some kind of middle-class someone with characteristics ranging from being bald, too hairy, spermy, impotent, omnipotent, etc.

Both have their charm and I don't see why I can't enjoy both for completely different reasons.

Saying 'Bollywood sucks' is roughly the same as mouthing a cliché like 'all politicians are crooks', though to convince people of the latter is considerably harder. Some of India sees Bollywood as film families, bullying, doing drugs and involved in non-inclusiveness and while that may be true, it's becoming less true every day. And you can't ignore movies like *Lootcase, Sherni, Kaagaz, Pagglait, Angrezi Medium, Bhonsle, Chhalaang* which also came out of this universe, in the above timeline.

I'm not saying the industry does not have issues (it does in plenty), but this black and white binary nonsense that is constantly perpetuated by social media is just a means to get retweets, not real conversation.

Let's talk about nepotism for a second.

Manoj Bajpai—arguably India's best actor right now—said that nepotism is there in every industry.[41] We can't keep on pretending that Bollywood is a unique phenomenon and the rest of the country comprises self-made people who didn't rely on their family name to get anywhere? We all owe something (personally I owe a lot) of our career to our parents—they

---

[41]'Manoj Bajpayee joins nepotism debate: 'This industry has wasted talent, in another country they would have been best actors', *Hindustan Times*, 24 June 2020, https://www.hindustantimes.com/bollywood/manoj-bajpayee-joins-nepotism-debate-this-industry-has-wasted-talent-in-another-country-they-would-have-been-best-actors/story-iw5nZYgNFILJkzJItAFlLL.html. Accessed on 10 February 2022.

should charge you tax on what they invested in you.

People speak against nepotism in Bollywood, but it is also true that 55 per cent of Indians have had arranged marriages.[42] You just used your nepotism to find yourself a mate and you judge when other people do it professionally? You have stores that are named 'Shah & Sons' and a majority of Indian businesses are run as a mini-monarchy passing on from parent to child, barring those children that decided to go get salaried jobs at Samsung, Dell, Hyundai, Ford, Reliance, Hinduja, The Aditya Birla Group, Nike—all of whom also happen to be family-run businesses.

Nepotism or family-run businesses are almost par for the course globally and also prevalent in every industry in India, but no one asks the Ambanis or Birlas or Tatas (not) to defend it.

If they did, this would be the conversation:

Journalist: 'Mr Mukesh, why is there nepotism in your company?'

Mukesh: 'Because it is our company. It's a family company.'

Journalist: 'But, what about all those strugglers—those hardworking start-ups and entrepreneurs—why can't they be CEO? Or chairman? Or MD?'

Mukesh: 'I am all of that.'

Journalist: 'That's nepotism—towards yourself!'

---

[42] Attri, Vibha. 'Telling Numbers: Indian youth marrying later, but traditional attitudes remain', *The Indian Express*, 2 June 2021, https://indianexpress.com/article/explained/explained-indian-youth-marrying-later-but-traditional-attitudes-remain-7331783/. Accessed on 2 March 2022.

Mukesh: 'Yes, it is our company. We are a merit-based organization for everything else. Everything else. Our CFO is not from the family for example.'

Journalist: 'But, why not CEO? Why not the lead role?'

Mukesh: 'Dude, it's our family company.'

Journalist: 'So, your company supports nepotism?'

Mukesh: 'In this one regard, yes.'

Next day: 'Non-Controversy: Mukesh supports nepotism!'

Response: Nobody cares. One retweet from KRK.

Next to next day: Newspaper bought out by industrialist.

Bollywood's issue has not been nepotism, it's the toxicity in the industry, which became a legit 'industry' barely a decade back. Fortunately, most of the toxicity lies with the previous generation of actors and directors that are now in their 50s and have to their credit understood their own toxicity. It reminds me of the Australian cricket team culture, which until Cameron Bancroft took sandpaper out of his undies (Google it—if you didn't know) was known for being a celebration of the alpha. The alphas were given a free pass because they were getting the wins under their belt. And it was considered that to be an alpha you have to push down all the betas to reiterate your status. Of course, in Bollywood, they pushed down the betas, not the *betas*. Thank you, thank you. I'm a professional comedian.

You'll hear stories of an older actor cutting with scissors another actor's shirt, slaps being exchanged like birthday gifts, bullying in the form of pranks, bullying in the form of bullying, ridiculous gender imbalances and worse—but, again, a lot of it probably lies in the past.

The best you can expect from people and an industry is a change for the better and I do believe the industry is doing exactly that, slowly but unsurely. Though, in their own occasionally twisted way, most of the changes are prompted by the market and will continue doing so.

People assume that the reason why Kangana is kind of correct (in this issue) is because so many Bollywood star kids kept denying their nepotism. For so long.

Except not all of them denied it. Some of them gave the correct answer like Ranbir Kapoor who once said, '…yes, honestly, it does exist.'[43] And Emraan Hashmi said, 'Yes, it exists and I got a break because of my uncle, Mahesh Bhatt.'[44] And nobody cared that they said it. Nobody. Similar statements by Sara Ali Khan, Shahid Kapoor and Sonam Kapoor were met with a similar response of nothingness. Someone accepting the truth and not denying it is rarely fun to report.

It's the perceived excuses which made the Siddhant Chaturvedi (*Gully Boy* actor and Mr Chaturvedi's son) and Ananya Panday (*SOTY-2* actress and Chunkey Panday's daughter) conversation go viral. In case you missed it, here's what happened—there was a round table chat including

---

[43]'When Ranbir Kapoor got talking about nepotism and said he would like to work hard for his children', *Pinkvilla*, 12 August 2020, https://www.pinkvilla.com/entertainment/news/when-ranbir-kapoor-got-talking-about-nepotism-and-said-he-would-work-hard-his-children-555943. Accessed on 15 February 2022.

[44]'Emraan Hashmi on nepotism: "I got a break because of my uncle Mahesh Bhatt"', *Firstpost*, 4 August 2017, https://www.firstpost.com/entertainment/bollywood/emraan-hashmi-on-nepotism-i-got-a-break-because-of-my-uncle-mahesh-bhatt-3893579.html. Accessed on 15 February 2022.

them and film critic, Rajeev Masand:

Rajeev Masand: What do you think of nepotism in Bollywood?

*Ananya (talks for three minutes about all sorts of things—I paraphrase her actual words for comedic effect and it annoys me significantly that I have to mention that this is paraphrased because some people will create a controversy if I mention that it is not)*: It's not so easy for us either. I have struggles. My dad is a great guy. He supports charities. It's not easy for me. Did you know my mother actually had to give birth to me? I had to come out myself. Also, a lot of times I have had to order food and feed myself. Do you know that us Bollywood star kids have to jet spray ourselves? Etc. Etc.

Siddhant Chaturvedi: '*Farak yeh hai jahaan humaare sapne poore hote hai waha inka struggle shuru hota hai* [The difference is where our dreams come true, their struggles start].'[45]

What he said was true. And people went insane shitting on Ananya Panday—which is not unexpected because it's rare that the Internet is empathetic toward anyone (including me as a troll and *a* trolled). The internet is only empathetic when it fits their agenda and/or world view and/or politics—if you don't fall under the same, then you can be crushed by an avalanche of bears and no one will bat an eyelid. So, the trolls came for her. Siddhant and Ananya did not seem to be genuinely affected by the exchange. Siddhant, in fact, seemed almost embarrassed by the virality of his statement, which kind of proves he made it on his own.

---

[45]'The Newcomers Roundtable 2019 with Rajeev Masand | Siddhant Chaturvedi, Ananya Panday, Tara Sutaria', CNN-News 18 YouTube, 31 December 2019, https://www.youtube.com/watch?v=O8BXjZQxAOk. Accessed on 15 February 2022.

Additionally, Chunky Panday did have an incredible career and definitely worked his ass off, so is it entirely unfathomable that his daughter would have a little leg up? The truth is that Ananya Panday is an easy target. Plus, she has 10 million followers on Instagram. That did not necessarily happen out of nepotism. People didn't follow her because her dad was really damn good in *Tezaab* (1988).

In fact, if so many people believe that she's proof of nepotism, then unfollow her, no? Unfollow all of them. All the Kapoors, Khans, Pandays, Ali Khans—unfollow them if you believe in nepotism so strongly. I will not because I don't follow them in the first place. Most of them seem like nice people and some are charming, good-looking, and that is always nice to see. #superficial. Some of them are also capable of saying dumb shit, especially about their circumstances, which they have been called out for. Fair enough.

The thing about most forms of entertainment—whether it's movies, music, comedy—is that the audience will not tolerate you for too long if you suck. You may get three movies (which is three movies more than someone significantly more talented), but post that you may as well start wishing for that call from Bigg Boss or if you're smart, start taking smaller roles and actually hone your craft.

However, the audience will reject you despite doing a movie (which was probably financed by your family) just because of your family history. Now, the viewer is monarch, unlike anytime before the Internet (2015—launch of Jio), where your options were limited. The film families gave you the films and you were forced to consume them because nothing else was there. Now, lots of other nothing else is there—so, you can choose the nothing you prefer and add nothing to the nothingness coming from them, if you choose to. Otherwise you can also do nothing.

One reason star kids get a leg-up is because all Bollywood kids hang out at the same parties, they keep meeting each other constantly, they're friends since childhood—obviously they'd want to work together. The closed circuit they have is a bit ridiculous and you can keep seeing it on their grams (that's the social media app, not a unit of measurement). So, if you're spending a year on a movie, you'd rather spend that time with someone you once shared a Jägermeister keg party with, which is how nepotism and networking works everywhere.

Over the last few years, the kind of people making it to these events and parties is a far more diverse crowd than ever before and it definitely needs to get more diverse. Even the biggest box office sellers of 2021 are not as dominated by nepotism as they were before, which means I still have a chance.

There are plenty of instances of ridiculously talented people being screwed over by the system. And that is truly terrible. There are some horrible stories of bullying which no one in their right mind can condone. However, there's also quite a few people that did not make it—not because of nepotism—because they had a bad attitude, they were socially inept, they didn't have good social media skills or just that they were not good enough.

A lot of them have given interviews and blamed nepotism for not being able to make it and you believe their narrative until you speak to the cast or the crew of films they were involved with and find out that no one enjoyed working with them because they were moody, rude, coked out or were stalking the assistant cameraperson.

The thing that drives me nuts is that many of the products of nepotism are (were?) given a considerably longer rope to misbehave, be unprofessional, be bullies and just be hard to work with because they were superstars or superstars' kids. But, that rope is now getting shorter. This does not apply to one particular superstar actor who has been all of those things for eons and whose rope is infinite, but that's another tale.

Who is this superstar? He's big. That's all, boss. I hope to work with him some day.

So, I agree that they've gotten a longer rope for eons, but that too is changing slowly. What doesn't make sense to me is this assumption that all you need in life is talent. 'I can't believe she didn't make it, she's so talented'—it really helps if you have talent and tenacity, but it definitely helps if you have talent, tenacity as well as social skills.

There continue to be plenty of cases of immensely talented people who didn't make it because preference was given to a star kid—but that's not the defining rule, especially not in 2021. Nepotism-based networking makes it considerably easier for star kids to break into mainstream Bollywood but given the tough circumstances, as an outsider you have to give yourself the best chance by networking as much as you can. I understand the anger, but if you don't know how to network or don't want to network and prefer sitting at home, hoping that Mr Bollywood will call you and say, 'Hey, you're talented, right? We heard it from your grandmother and four of your friends. No, you don't need to audition or hang out with us and build a bond. Just hearing you're talented is enough for us. Your shoot for a ₹100-crore film, where you're being paid ₹98 crore, starts tomorrow because you're so talented and deserve nothing less.'

I've met Shahrukh Khan twice in my life and before I met him, I was not a fan. After I met him, I would consider donating my beautiful bum to him—if he needs it, probably as a foot rest. The man has charm oozing out of him, he also has tremendous people skills and a terrific sense of humour—you feel motivated after meeting him. On the other hand, there's some people you meet from Bollywood that make you want to watch 12 hours of anime to purify yourself from their uncreative stench.

Forget Bollywood, look at normal life: if you don't go for your office party, if you don't spend time getting to know your colleagues, helping them, having a drink with them and maintaining good relations with them because you want to—not because there's something in it for you—then don't sit and shout about how you didn't make it because of some mystical reason.

I know I haven't done that enough, which is why I haven't been on an OTT platform in four years. Or maybe I just suck, it's possible. But, don't tell me yet—let me figure it out myself.

A lot of the time I hear stories of people not even being called for these events on the basis of their family background (or lack thereof), their gender or something equally ridiculous, and that genuinely sucks. If you want to make an effort to be a star, consider hanging out with a bunch of idiots to get ahead—it's the way in most industries.

It also raises the question: do you even want to be a star? But, that's a separate question.

In the last two years, Bollywood has seen a mix of nepotism and no-connection in the top ranks. In no particular order, my favorite people in Bollywood include Irrfan Khan, Manoj Bajpai, Anurag Kashyap, Ayushmann Khurrana, Alia

Bhatt, Ranveer Singh, Zoya Akhtar, Pankaj Tripathi, Boman Irani, Saif Ali Khan, Rajkummar Rao, Naseeruddin Shah (whenever he emerges again), Neeraj Ghaywan, Rajkumar Hirani, Tabu, Aamir Khan, Vishal Bhardwaj, Rahi Barve and Anand Gandhi—the last two directed my favourite movie of the last three years, *Tumbbad*. That's a pretty mixed bag right there. Though, why would you put them in a bag?

Now, let me list my favourite industrialists: Ratan Tata, Narayana Murthy, Kumar Mangalam Birla, Azim Premji are all I can remember. Isn't that sad? I remember Bollywood stars more than I remember industrialists. And even in the above list, 50 per cent is 'nepotism'. List your favourite politicians, if you have any. I don't. But, if you did, you can bet your ass (why would you? You need that ass for many things like donating to SRK in case he needs it) that at least 50 per cent of them will be products of nepotism.

The only industries with bare nepotism are mid-level jobs, probably sports and dare I say it, comedy. This is because the industry is young and probably won't last beyond this generation.

Also, in my limited encounters with them, these beneficiaries of nepotism in Bollywood work ridiculously hard. Most of them sleep five hours a day and are working out for the remaining 19 hours. The reason why 'some' of them are surface level actors is because their life experience has not extended beyond achieving 2 per cent body fat—but that's another thing.

A lot of these people have literally been trained their whole life to be stars. Please note: it does not necessarily mean they've been trained to be actors. And it also does not mean that I think they're all great and worth defending. A lot of them have been dogshit for years—it is admirable that they've maintained consistency.

Now that I've been (relatively) nice to the star power people, let's talk about what they've done wrong and oh so wrong.

Award ceremonies seem to be the platform where the hate towards them inflates. Every year, the Filmfare Awards will incite a controversy over winners—and it's ALWAYS the same two categories: Best Debut Male and Best Debut Female. In 2020, the winner was Ananya Panday (Chunky Panday's daughter) and Abhimanyu Dassani (Bhagyashree's son—actually good). People were outraged just like every year. What no one acknowledges is that the category itself is a celebration of nepotism. Since I'm a stats man, I did the research. Since 1989 when the two awards were launched, here are the stats for the winners:[46]

Best Debut (Male): 1989–2020
Won by Nepotism: 17
Not Won by Nepotism: 9

Best Debut (Female): 1989–2020
Won by Nepotism: 10
Not Won by Nepotism: 17

This means that of 53 awards, 27 have been won because of Bollywood family planning, i.e., '*hum do humaare co-stars* [Us two and our co-stars].' This forms a percentage of 50.9, which also happens to be the percentage of nepotism-based guests on

---

[46]'Filmfare Best Male Debut Awards', *NetTV4u*, https://nettv4u.com/entertainment/hindi/article/filmfare-best-male-debut-awards. Accessed on 15 February 2022.

*Koffee with Karan*. Yes, I did the stats for that also (till 2020). Fifty per cent. I really need to get a job with cricinfo.com.

With *Koffee with Karan*, I get why the numbers would be that high—he's hanging out with all these film folk all the time and having hosted my own version of an interview show, getting people outside your own little circle is genuinely tough work. I don't agree with the numbers, but I understand them.

Side note: The Best Debut (Female) in 1991 was won by Pooja Bhatt for a movie called *Daddy*. Yes. Directed by her father. The title is why she won. Ironically, she actually deserved the award, but that's still a weird wink to the audience. And in 1998, Akshaye Khanna (another deserved winner) won for *Himalay Putra* (son of the Himalayas). The subtleties are too unsubtle.

Nepotism exists in Bollywood. It also exists everywhere else. However, the gap between nepotism and credit is shortening rapidly. Since the late 2010s, the star kids have been getting better (barring exceptions) and the public dictates who they want and who they don't. Or at least they should instead of complaining.

This is why I like being a comedian. There is no nepotism. We wait for our kids to grow up before we can 'launch' them—except that the audience will not listen to them beyond five minutes if they are not funny. If Alia Bhatt (she's good) did stand-up and was not funny, there would be a limit to how much people could fake their interest. Laughter is usually earned, not given, unless you're paid to sit and do it which is another essay on Indian TV. #ArchanaPuranSidhu.

I'll leave you with this quote by Vidya Balan, 'I am bored with this discussion on nepotism. I mean I am seriously bored on who is on which side of the debate these days.'[47]

Yeah, it might be better for Bollywood to correct other pressing problems like why they had to make two movies on bald guys (*Bala* and *Ujda Chaman*) and I was not approached to be the lead role in either.

## Solution

The problem for Bollywood is the denial and the overt celebration of nepotism. And even though the current generation does not flaunt their family connections, they should all learn from Indian politics.

Denial examples: Saif Ali Khan is one of my favourite actors (no jokes) because he makes interesting choices and executes them well—from playing Langda Tyaagi in *Omkara* and Sartaj Singh in *Sacred Games* to working in *Go Goa Gone*, *Kaalakaandi* and pretending Kareena and him using an Airbnb[48] (I actually do—so please pay me for an ad, Airbnb). But him talking about nepotism is a role he's played with a bit of 'struggle'.

First, Varun Dhawan, Karan Johar and he screamed, 'Nepotism Rocks' at IIFA 2017.[49] Kangana took offense to

---

[47]IANS, 'I am bored with this discussion on nepotism:Vidya Balan', *Hindustan Times*, 25 July 2017, https://www.hindustantimes.com/bollywood/i-am-bored-with-this-discussion-on-nepotism-vidya-balan/story-ToEInDJsOJworuDVZR61qI.html. Accessed on 9 February 2022.

[48]'Who helped Saif & Kareena book their Airbnb home?', *YouTube*, 20 June 2018, https://www.youtube.com/watch?app=desktop&v=mb3sX8NnahM. Accessed on 9 February 2022.

[49]'DNA Exclusive: Saif Ali Khan pens an open letter over the 'Nepotism rocks' brouhaha during IIFA 2017', *DNA*, 21 July 2017, https://www.dnaindia.com/bollywood/report-saif-ali-khan-pens-an-open-letter-over-the-neopitism-rocks-brouhaha-during-iifa-2017-2508860. Accessed on 10 February 2022.

this. Saif spoke about eugenics (which everyone googled and figured out had significant connections to Nazi scientists and then consequently became outraged) and then said he apologized to Kangana and doesn't owe anyone else an apology. Fine, that's his call. He definitely does not need to apologize to me because I enjoyed that moment at IIFA. It was awkward and great, every one of these award ceremonies could use some spicing up. It rescues us from the drudgery of watching celebrities suck each other off for six hours.

Every award ceremony should have such a moment. Some recommendations:

- Filmfare 2022: Salman gets on stage and screams, 'Blackbucks are my boyfriends,' while Sooraj Barjatya politely claps.
- Zee Cine Awards 2022: Sajid Khan gets on stage and says, 'I got on this stage by sleeping with myself. And I didn't enjoy it,' while Ashutosh Gowariker screams at him about not respecting India's most respected man, Ashutosh Gowariker.
- National Awards 2021: Sonakshi Sinha is just walking around aimlessly muttering to herself, 'Honestly, what am I doing here?'
- IIFA 2022: Hrithik Roshan gets on stage and says he wants to talk about the emails exchanged between Kangana and him adding that it's just a PPT of email forwards of hundreds of Garfield comic strips.

I'm a little embarrassed by the number of times I've made jokes on Sonakshi, Hrithik, Kangana and the rest of the Hindi film industry. Truth is that Bollywood is an easy target because they make themselves so. The BJP continues to go on and on about Congress' dynastic ways and yet so many tickets are offered on Vodafone Family+Friends Quota in the BJP.[50] Everyone is an idealist until opportunity arises and then you are a hypocrite. Them, you, me, us.

People would think about voting for Gopinath Munde's daughter because they liked him so they kind of like her. It's the same reason people would watch *SOTY-2*, but maybe not watch *SOTY-3* if they didn't like *SOTY-2*, or may not vote for Pankaja Munde the second time if she doesn't do a good job the first time. And, yes I just compared *Student of the Year* to Maharashtra politics—give me a Pulitzer already.

Nepotism opens doors, but consumers can close them if they don't like you—that's the rule in all industries. It's definitely true in politics, the only difference being the lead actor in the BJP biopic is not based on nepotism—and that's where the debate ends for them. The problem for the Congress is that everyone knows their lead actor is a result of nepotism and he/she keeps the movie franchise of Congress running and replacing their Ananya Panday with someone else who would even further wipe out their box office earnings.

Bollywood should learn from Indian politics and how star kids in the political scene deal with questions of acceptance and patriotism.

If someone says, 'Hey you got this chance because of your parent?', always answer, 'Yes he/she was a great person and I'm happy to carry their legacy and I count myself very lucky to serve this great nation of ours—India!'

---

[50]'Tickets to Family in UP, Uttarakhand Raises Rebellion in BJP', News 18, 23 January 2017, https://www.news18.com/news/politics/tickets-to-family-raises-rebellion-in-bjp-1339675.html. Accessed on 10 February 2022.

'Do you think there's nepotism in politics?'

'Yes, there is and we consider ourselves very lucky and will not take this opportunity lightly to serve our great nation of India! Coincidentally, I hear there's not going to be any water supply in your area and I don't know why…'

Acceptance and not celebrating your nepotism and giving veiled threats is the right way to deal with it—you're welcome, Bollywood.

## small thoughts

I was discussing with some friends about satire in India and we came to the wonderful conclusion that there's not really any satire in India, at the moment.

There's probably a couple of news-based YouTubers, a few podcasters and a handful of cartoonists who still attempt to push the line. And the line keeps pushing back at them and every few weeks there will be some issue facing one of them—either official, unofficial or pretending to be either.

I used to work for an attempted satire show where we could cover a bunch of topics, but you were not allowed to name people directly for the fear of offending them, their fans, their sycophants and also getting cases filed by people looking for ways to misuse our laws.

So, Aishwarya Rai became Caishwarya Gai, Manmohan Singh was Punmohan Singh, Atal Bihari Vajpayee was Atul Vihari Bajpai, Shahrukh Khan was Rukhrukh Khan, Salman Khan was Solomon Khan, etc. These are names I remember, probably incorrectly, but the fact that you could not and still can not make fun of anyone on mainstream Indian TV or radio is telling.

There is no mainstream satire in India and maybe that in itself is a piece of satire in itself—can the non-existence of satire be the ultimate expression of satire? Maybe the greatest satirists are the people that have set an environment to create no satire, maybe they have just eliminated all competition—after all, they are significantly advanced comedians, creating satire that will be appreciated after its time.

I know what this book was supposed to be and what it became out of fear—so, there's that.

# 13

## *Cancel Woke Culture?*

### April 2021

It's mandatory that comedians talk about woke people and cancel culture at least once a week. It's mandated by law and if I were to not write this piece, I'd be ostracized from the community as well as the Council of Predictability, which takes care of other predictabilities, such as divisive politics, having way more than one drink when you said, 'Just one drink, okay?', not getting any sleep on the night before your 6.00 a.m. flight, news anchors screaming when they don't have a point, China not accepting blame, America not accepting blame, any country not accepting blame, injustice and how your ugliest photos on Instagram will get the most likes.

Anyway, let's go down this path of predictability…

The term 'woke' is attributed to the African-American fight for racial equality. Now it applies to a lot of other things and people. So, technically everyone who is not African-American who calls themselves woke is guilty of cultural appropriation, which is not very woke. So, go to sleep, or slope.

It's really easy to dismiss woke culture as a bunch of snowflakes that melt in the wind and eat organically sourced soya for breakfast, then pet an endangered animal on the head after asking for permission while writing a tweet thread about the sun not understanding the damage it has caused to Earth.

## A Sample

'The sun may be the creator of life and provide food to plants or whatever, but it's highly problematic how it shamelessly causes skin cancer, drying of oceans and deserts, while fueling a hat industry that probably uses child labour in South East Asian countries. 1/906.'

'Yes, we must look at the advantages of solar energy, and photosynthesis is probably a good thing, but the sun has been getting away with so much for millions of years.'

P.S.: It also did very little to prevent dinosaurs from being killed by asteroids. 2/906.'

'The sun has all these gases and things—so, why couldn't it just fire an ultraviolet ray to save the endangered Diplodocus? Not to forget, melting our ice caps to cause global warming? Is this okay? Enough is enough. #CancelTheSun #BlockTheSun 3/906.'

'Ultraviolet? More like ultraviolent. #SunBlock2022 4/906.'

I would have written all 906 tweets, but I am not outraged at the sun because there's usually two sides to a story. But, there really is not these days.

Raging against woke culture without entirely understanding it is essentially similar to opposing the hippies in the '60s as hairy acid lovers that wore really great T-shirts. Every generation has a movement of young people trying to make a change and institute some form of idealism. They also involve some shape of drugs and tons of sex, but that's just young people. Being idealistic is not a bad thing, expecting the world to be better is not. And it could be argued that 'woke' folk have brought about or attempted to bring about significant change to the world around them.

Look at the circumstances this generation finds themselves in: there's a global housing crisis, a global job crisis, a global climate crisis, a global war crisis, a globe-wide crisis from people believing these are not general global crises. And a large chunk of youngsters want the world to get better so that they can continue living in it. There's a chunk of young people who are completely out of their minds, but that happens in every generation and in every movement.

There is a chunk that accuses people of bullying them and then bullies the people they've accused of bullying—intent be damned. There is a chunk that shove isms on people for words that were either misconstrued, misinterpreted or retracted. There is a chunk that is never satisfied with any apology and would prefer the person in question ceases to exist or do anything. There is also a chunk that believes in different rules for different people without realizing they're doing it. There's a chunk that believes McDonalds' toys for BTS should only go to BTS fans. There's a chunk that does not allow any leeway in how tight they want other people's speech to be, but will still talk about freedom of speech while contradicting themselves on the freedom of other people's speech. And more.

But, for every such chunk, there's a smarter and genuinely empathetic block of genuine young people fighting against racism, gender inequalities, casteism, abuse of power, global warming and more. There's also a lot of young people that say nothing and do not vilify people because they understand how complex people's decisions are, and you are allowed to do that. There's also a lot of young people that are drunk and in their own world and that's fine as well.

I'm surprised some of these young people aren't just going out there on a daily basis burning buildings and banks while hacking into every billionaire's accounts and transferring that money to pay off their debts: both current and future. Please don't do that. I'm not suggesting anything of the sort. Though such movements are happening globally, I don't condone them. I'm not going to stand on Capitol Hill and say, 'I love you guys.'

This is the world young people have inherited. A world that seems to be in financial, spiritual and environmental debt. They're essentially thinking: what possible way will we die? Will it be a tsunami? Poverty? Another global pandemic (which experts say is likely to happen)? Cannibalism due to food shortage? Food shortage due to cannibalism? Global warming? An ice age? Chinese debt falling on your head? What?

And this is not unusual for humanity. We seem to put one generation in a place of continuous threat probably once every century—but this is the first of that generation to have social media. So, obviously they will rage! Because they have the platform and they have a cause: their own existence.

Swiftly getting into hacky comedy territory: if a variant of social media had existed during the 1904 plague in India, the Great Depression or the many invasions of India, the tweets would probably have been about as angry, with a few less ads because those eras had far less start-ups and back then the start-ups were actual countries.

A lot of older people may not realize this because they

aren't going to be around for most of the end of the world. And even though I don't plan to be around for too long, I wonder what kind of world will be left for my children. I am aiming to get them started on a diet of insects and also get them familiarized with the terrain of Mars, just to ensure that they are prepared for what might lie ahead.

So, if you're woke or just angry, I do understand your rage. A lot of it. Some of it. Not all.

What I don't understand is how *you* don't understand that occasionally there can be misunderstandings. There can also be people having shitty days. There can be people saying things they don't agree with anymore. I'm not sure what idealistic worldview allows you to imagine that people are constantly angelic and in control of their emotions. People are capable of making mistakes and they're also capable of correcting them. And also an accusation doesn't imply conviction because you rule out a very simple thing called perception.

Here's a few examples of the same:

I was at the airport taking a flight to Melbourne for a series of sold-out shows at the Melbourne cricket ground. It might also have been a flight to Jamshedpur to perform for 60 Marwaris, I can't remember. There was a lady arguing with the ground staff at the boarding gate. I had 15 minutes before my boarding started, so I sat down with my coffee to see if I needed to intervene and calm things down as I have a very trustworthy face. But, it was mainly to see if I could find some material for my stand-up show that night.

The lady was arguing about the size of her handbag, which was the size of the lady herself (this is not fat shaming—it's just that the bag was big, not her). The ground staff, talking to her, said, 'No worries, Ma'am. Please leave this with us and you can collect it as check-in baggage upon landing. The lady was not satisfied and pointing at her handbag (that could have managed to fit her family) said it was under 7 kg, which could have been true had kilogram become a new term for metric tons. I'm pretty sure I saw the trunk of an elephant peek out from inside the bag.

This went on for a couple of minutes and the lady was raging as if she was losing a news debate. So, the Central Industrial Security Force (CISF) went up to her and told her politely to calm down. She didn't. They asked her to move to the side. This angered her further. They said they may have to make her miss her flight because she was being unruly and said they would need to recheck her bag. The lady lay down on the floor, touching the CISF's shoes and sarcastically said, 'What do you want me to do—touch your feet?' She didn't need to use a sarcastic tone because she was already touching the CISF lady's feet. That's a misplaced use of sarcasm, but that wasn't the worst of it.

Now, I know plenty of airports across the world where this kind of behaviour would have you arrested. But, due credit to the CISF personnel who maintained their composure while this lady raged. Her rage only abated when they told her she would be banned from flying (no, her surname was not Kamra)—and then she 'allowed' her handbag to be checked in. It required 12 men in a tractor to carry it forward.

Anyway, situation was defused—big deal. I spoke about this lady in the show at night—whichever city it was, Melbourne, Jamshedpur, Ranchi, Chernobyl, I don't remember.

Cut to a few days later, someone from the audience of that day's show shared an Instagram post with me about the same lady! I've changed the name of the airline because I can't remember which one it was. Here's roughly what she said, 'Never flying Purple Spice Air again. I was at the airport where I was humiliated by the ground staff for the size of my bag, which no one had a problem with till I reached the gate. Is this how you treat your fliers, Purple? Did you have to call the police on me? Disgusting, humiliated.'

There were almost a hundred comments accusing Purple Spice Air of ill-treating her, with others sharing their stories of dealing with Purple Air, etc. I tracked her post for a day, contemplating intervening on behalf of the CISF and the ground staff whose names were being sullied and hopefully getting free flights from Purple Spice Air, when they replied to her post, 'Ma'am, sorry to hear about your experience, we take customer relations very seriously. We have raised the issue and will speak to all concerned persons and go through the CCTV footage to ensure we get to the bottom of this.' Lo and behold, the lady deleted the post.

If there was no CCTV footage, some unfortunate CISF personnel may have been reprimanded or punished for what that lady was convinced was not her fault.

Perception. It's something that gets lost between a social media post and what actually happened because all of us remember things differently. I've witnessed many people recount the chain of events from a terrible day in a completely different way from how they actually unfolded. Here's another non-controversial one.

A man I was following on LinkedIn was absolutely disgusted with a Zomato (the food delivery app) customer service executive. He had posted a screenshot of his conversation with the man.

Man: My food was 35 minutes late.

Customer care: My sincerest apologies, Sir. Sorry you had to go through that.

Man: You cannot treat your customers like this. It was 45 minutes late.

Customer care: Really sorry, Sir. We will talk to the delivery executive.

Man: Absolutely horrible. How can you be 55 minutes late? You guys should not make promises you can't keep!

Customer care: Okay.

The man's post was about how the customer care executive had the audacity, the daring, the gumption to tell him, 'Okay'. His post was all about being ill-treated and how Zomato should shut down if they didn't know how to deal with their customers. The post got HUNDREDS of people outraged—not sure what exchange they saw, but they all vented against Zomato, ignoring the fact that the customer care apologized THREE times. What else is the person supposed to do? Lie down and touch the man's feet? (Bad example.)

And, not to forget the case of the lady in Bengaluru who accused a Zomato delivery man of punching her over delayed service.[51] The man was on the verge of losing his job and had to come on the news to tearfully explain that that's not what happened—the lady owed him money and was refusing to

---

[51] 'Zomato delivery executive punches Bengaluru woman after altercation for THIS reason', Zee News, 10 March 2021, https://zeenews.india.com/viral/zomato-delivery-executive-punches-bengaluru-woman-after-altercation-for-this-reason-2346996.html. Accessed on 2 March 2022.

accept the parcel because it was late. The police investigated the case and I'm not sure what even happened there—news only lasts till there is an accusation in place and not when the actual justice is being meted out.

Public perception on the case shifted wildly in either direction, eventually settling on the delivery man and his tearful clarification. Now, imagine a scenario where the delivery man had not cried on a news channel. Imagine if he dealt with his emotions differently and denied the allegations with a straight face. Imagine if he remained stoic. Would public perception then have shifted in his favour?

The answer is probably no. No one can say with certainty what happened in the case. While the evidence points in one direction, it all melts down to perception. People who are able to express their emotions and do so loudly and repeatedly are always deemed to be correct—which is absurd. They're plenty of people who don't know how or why to do that and they are immediately seen as the guilty party.

Anyway, when someone wants to cancel an individual, a company, a TV show or whatever, they seem to rule out intent, perception, changes in behaviour, etc. And we have a human instinct to always support the underdog. If the power dynamics are lopsided towards one side, then that's the side we tend to support. If they have power, they're assumed to be wrong. Underdogs can perceptively do no wrong—which is why we support New Zealand cricket.

When I go through comments of a post where someone is banned, cancelled, suspended or even called out for something that they said nine years back, I see two kinds of people: those who agree and those who disagree. And it might be that those who disagree said something 'problematic' nine years back on social media and those who agree are people who have forgotten that they said something 'problematic' nine years back.

There are many of my stand-ups, tweets, thoughts and opinions from the past that make me cringe while I think about them. *Who was that jackass? What the hell was he even trying to say? Is he a moron? I can reassure you—yes, he was.* I apologize for all of it, to whoever it may concern, which is a lot of people.

I've deleted a lot of things from the Internet because I did not agree with them. They were atrocious or dumb or had at least one line that was precisely that—jokes I should have worked on longer, jokes I should have run past more people, jokes that I should have known better. You're constantly trying to know better and that's a luxury and benefit of doubt I also accord to other people—and I do feel most people accord the same to other people as well. Most people.

I read a quote somewhere that said, 'The best kind of apology is a change in behaviour', which makes sense. The problem with the Internet is that it's a pretty big place. And it has corners and crevices that you discover daily. Every day, I discover something on the Internet which makes me think, 'Oh I did not know that', or 'They do it like that also?'

But the hugeness of the Internet means people can't necessarily 'see' your change in behaviour unless you display it precisely. You could display your change of behaviour for years on YouTube (for example) or on stage and some people on LinkedIn will still think, 'They're that same piece of shit from 2011 because I have not bothered to follow up on their career, their words and their output ever since then and until they display their change of behaviour right here, right under my nose on my LinkedIn feed, they have not changed at all! Looking beyond this specific part of the Internet is hard work—so, let's not even give another human a chance.'

Here's a question: what is the purpose of calling someone out for their words from their past? Unless it's for something that is truly criminal, is it that you want them to do better, improve, make amends? Have you checked if they have? Do you want to get all of us aligned as people to a point where we—WE—together get to a point of coexistence and understanding. Or do you want them to just not be able to do anything anymore ever again? If you want someone to be better, it's conceivable that you too may need to be so.

Also, you're allowed to exist in a world with differing opinions. You're allowed to have more than one angle to any topic. Otherwise, I believe the Earth is flat and you must agree.

By the way, if you have been called out for something you said ages ago and you've apologized and everything seems to imply that your apology is genuine, let's move on.

People are capable of evolving and most of us are four intelligent conversations away from reaching a place of understanding, if not agreement. Maybe we all need a little patience with other people's unintended ignorance. Patience is a real pain in the ass and it often requires repetition, but it seems the only real way to change perception and 'problematic' behaviour. Otherwise, we are just groups of beings constantly splitting into binary worlds that loathe, call out and refuse to understand each other because we've decided who we are and who our enemy is, and that doesn't seem very woke.

## Solution

School kids from the age of nine need to be taught about social media. Physics may help you understand refraction and inspire a career in the sciences, but learning not to treat social media like a chalkboard for nonsensical thoughts when you're young will help you not get fired from your job at CERN because you called your best friend a slur on TikTok in 2023. Or it could also be a lesson in teaching people empathy and helping them understand that terrible people do exist in the world and should be fought. But, not every single person that you see/perceive with a target painted on their back is some kind of -ist. Sometimes people make mistakes and your virtue signaling to indicate how you called them out so you're a better person than them can occasionally make you come off as a bit of a turd, and also, a lot more inflexible than the person you're accusing.

    I know this because I've been on both sides of that turd pile. I've been the turd and been accused by one. So I know how it smells in either direction.

P.S.: I'm sorry I used the word t*** up there. If you're reading this in 2025, when that word for some reason has some -ist overtones, I sincerely apologize. I'm a bit of a t*** myself.

## small thoughts

*Whenever I go out for a lunch or dinner with my wife or sister, the third most critical thing (after ordering the food and finding a parking spot within 100 km of the venue in Mumbai) is always the photos. I personally have started hating taking photos at any of these outings, though I will shamelessly use their photos on my own social media after whining about it for 10 minutes.*

*Some of my favourite memories of travel or any outings are stored inside this incredible storage device called my brain. My brain does not remember much, but it does remember some great images.*

*While social media has allowed an incredible amount of entertaining content, it has also led to a unique combination of narcissism and anxiety. We need photos and videos of ourselves because we love ourselves so much (especially in 12 MPs) and are consistently afraid that the world does not love us as much as we love ourselves (2,000 likes is not enough love).*

*If you're drinking a lot of alcohol, it's in your best interest to at least ensure you skip three days in a week. Maybe we (you, me) should apply the same rule to social media, even if for three hours a day. That's what I do with alcohol.*

*Take a break, let your ego and your narcissism breathe a bit.*

# 14

## *China is World*

*This was written in April 2020, which is worth noting because so much has changed and so much is still the same and time moves like an unforgiving concept.*

China is currently in territorial disputes with 18 countries,[52] despite being bordered by just 14 countries. So, they are currently in border disputes with countries that don't even touch China. This basic factoid was tweeted by me and then made it to prime time news as the opening statement of no less than three news anchors—which also proves that we've reached a point where an idiot comedian does more basic research than some journalists. But, we've already covered that.

Obviously the prime reason for these disputes is the sea. Essentially, China believes the sea and the ocean is part of China because technically every water drop on Earth has at some stage touched a part of China or has been touched by a Chinese citizen and that's enough basis for claiming the

---

[52]'It's not just India, China has border disputes with 18 countries. Here's the list', India TV, 26 June 2020, https://www.indiatvnews.com/fyi/india-china-border-dispute-with-18-countries-south-china-sea-india-border-ladakh-629333. Accessed on 22 February 2022.

sea(s)—which should belong to other countries. The basis of these disputes is roughly as follows:

- A country—say Philippines—draws a nautical map saying this part of the sea is theirs.
- Another country—say Vietnam—says this other part is theirs.
- Another country—say Indonesia, Malaysia, Brunei—also say this other part is theirs.
- China says nautical maps in China are different from those of other countries because Chinese maps are best and so all the other countries are wrong and the parts of the sea that China says are China's are China's because China said so.
- An arbitrational tribunal—set up by, let's say, United
- Nations Convention on the Law of the Sea—rules AGAINST China.
- China disagrees with the tribunal because neither the United Nations, nor any of the other countries have naval forces that are larger than China's, so once again China is correct. (Please note: disagreeing with a tribunal and then proceeding to do whatever you want to do is next level genius and also raises the point and power of having a tribunal whose ruling can be voided by merely 'disagreeing' with it, if you have the power. It's akin to stealing a horse from your neighbour and then disagreeing with the CCTV footage because you're richer than the judge who ruled you're guilty.)
- China builds naval islands in the disputed parts of the sea and by 'sea law' (not a technical term), the

disputed parts are no more disputed...because look we got an island here which had magically appeared. So, everyone else STFU and go watch *Pirates of the Caribbean: At World's End*.
- It also doesn't help that you can't make a border on the sea because it would just float away—not that borders concern China much. Borders are merely suggestions or a yellow light at a traffic signal when visible from China and a red light at a traffic signal when viewed from any other country in the world (barring USA and occasionally India).

This is a great tactic and works wonderfully well for China. The other tactic is also loans, here's how that goes:

- China lends money to a country that doesn't have money—let's say, Sri Lanka, Zambia, Nigeria, an island in Maldives and possibly 20 more countries—to build a port or a dam.
- The receiving country is excited. 'Look, we got a dam,' they say. Someone asks, 'Who gave the money?' They say, 'STFU, our country is great. We got a dam. Don't make me drown you.' Years later, China asks, 'Our dear beloved friend, would you by any chance have money to pay off the loan?' The receiving country is shocked, appalled. They forgot that loans have to be paid back. Bribes may have been paid to important officials to conveniently forget this minor oversight. Country says, 'Damn, we don't really have the money. What shall we do now?'
- China is an accommodating lender and says, 'Friend, do not worry. We are your friend. Let's say that dam/

port/building/area around it is now ours. Let's say we keep it on a lease of 99 years—a completely original idea that we definitely did not borrow from the British.'
- The country heaves a sigh of relief—after all, it's just a dam. Who cares who owns this dam in our country? They think a bit deeper and realize they still don't have the money to build a port. They once again ask China, 'Hey, can we have money for a port as well?'
- And before the country realizes, buildings, infrastructure, critically important parts are suddenly owned by something called PRC (short form: Pretty Rad Cool guys).

It's genuinely impressive how smartly China executes this and how subtly countries keep falling for this debt trap. If you look at it neutrally—and as an Indian it is considerably hard to do so—it's a genius tactic. Conquerors in the past used wars and soldiers and military prowess to conquer lands—until East India Company came in and changed the game. As William Dalrymple[53] points out, it was a company that ruled a country. And they did so by using trade, bribes, division, loans and the threat of death and slavery. It's a horrible tactic, but a successful one and for that China owes a debt (pardon the pun) to the British.

Then there is the third tactic and India should feel 'special' that this particularly is largely used for her. We're familiar

---

[53] Jasanoff, Maya. 'The Anarchy by William Dalrymple review – the East India Company and corporate excess', *The Guardian,* 11 September 2019, https://www.theguardian.com/books/2019/sep/11/anarchy-relentless-rise-east-india-company-william-darymple-review. Accessed on 9 February 2022.

with the tactic, it's a border kabaddi. They come towards our border, give us 'hull' (meaning a mild threat in Hindi—not ship) and then bugger off and pretend like nothing happened, or maybe pretend that what happened was okay because the world is owned by China.

They've been playing border kabaddi for decades with not pleasant results—and then of course came the most unpleasant result which was Galwan. China objected to Indian road construction at Galwan River, which flows from the disputed Aksai Chin region to Ladakh[54]—an objection that made little sense given the river's flow. The 'skirmish' that followed led to the death of 20 Indian officers and 43 Chinese soldiers as per international and Indian reports—or 20 Indian officers and five Chinese soldiers as per some Chinese reports or 81 Indian soldiers and zero Chinese soldiers as per other Chinese reports or there was a skirmish caused by India and China resolved it with magnanimous non-violence as per one Chinese report (that I'm sure exists).

To drive the point home, the incident was covered heavily across all Indian media and completely ignored by Chinese media, which may go on to prove in whose favour the skirmish went. The details of the skirmish were horrific: since firearms are not allowed in the region, the soldiers fought with boulders, rods and clubs with barb wire on them, a terribly gory image akin to the climax of *The Walking Dead*.

The repercussions of this in India was immediate with—not for the first time—Indians deciding to #BoycottChina. It's

---

[54]Krishnan, Ananth. 'The Hindu Explains | Who does Galwan Valley belong to?', *The Hindu*, 22 June 2020, https://www.thehindu.com/news/national/the-hindu-explains-who-does-galwan-valley-belong-to/article31879418.ece. Accessed on 16 February 2022.

a stance that many Indians took and it's beyond someone like me to comment on whether it's right or wrong. If you listen to Sonam Wangchuk (a celebrated Indian scientist, resident of Ladakh and briefly Aamir Khan) or an Indian soldier at the border, it's a bit hard to not pay heed to calls for Indian boycott of Chinese goods.

However, the on-ground battle of Indian customers and retailers struggling with finances in COVID-19 times (and in general times) stands in the way. It's a bit hard in these tough times (or most times) to coerce someone, who is barely making ends meet, to not purchase a cheaper product or opt for a cheaper producer. So, as far as I can see it, it is your own decision.

Side note: As things eventually panned out, of course, trade between India and China in 2021 continued to move at full speed or close to it because what other option is there?

Anyway, as happens with everything in India, the #BoycottChina movement immediately led to the ridiculous. Indians who had bought Chinese TVs threw them out of their windows and smashed them, which makes you doubt who is winning in that regard? You've already bought the TV and given money to a Chinese manufacturer—how is smashing a new TV teaching a lesson? Unless you smashed a China-made TV that was bought by a Chinese person that you stole—that would be a considerably tougher option.

There was even a viral video of two young girls smashing their Chinese phones with hammers and throwing it off their terrace.[55] While the sentiment may be understandable, the

---

[55] https://www.youtube.com/watch?v=AOwMvHuA69Y. Accessed on 2 March 2022.

practicality of it leaves a lot to be fathomed. A phone is a pretty heavy thing to fling off a balcony and you don't want to injure (or worse) a fellow Indian while trying to prove a point to the Chinese. In that instance of someone dying because of a flying phone, that phone may well be identified as a Chinese weapon. Additionally, you've already bought the phone, so use it, why waste it?

One of my favourite actors, Arshad Warsi (I genuinely like the guy) had the best intentions, but might have had not so good an execution. He tweeted, 'I am consciously going to stop using everything that is Chinese. As they are a part of most of the things we use, it will take time, but I know one day I'll be Chinese free. You should try it too...'[56] The only flaw in his plan was that right under his tweet it read, 'Twitter for iPhone'. As you may be aware, the Internet is a wonderfully kind and sweet place and no one trolled Arshad at all on this foible. Let's leave it at that.

Then there is the case of Republican Party of India leader and Minister of State for Social Justice and Empowerment in the current government, Ramdas Athawale who said, 'China is a country that betrays. In India, all Chinese products must be boycotted. Chinese food and restaurants that sell Chinese food should be closed down in India.'[57]

We will stop eating their cuisine and that shall in a

---

[56]Arshad Warsi tweet, https://twitter.com/ArshadWarsi/status/1266660927354494977?s=20. Accessed on 1 March 2022.
[57]Chaturvedi, Anumeha. 'Minister's call to ban Chinese food 'bizarre', say Indian restaurants', *The Economic Times*, 19 June 2020, https://economictimes.indiatimes.com/news/politics-and-nation/boycott-products-made-in-china-close-down-restaurants-selling-chinese-food-ramdas-athawale/articleshow/76442945.cms?from=mdr. Accessed on 9 February 2022.

spiritual sense defeat the Chinese. One fine day, the Chinese minister of food home delivery shall wake up and feel queasy, 'Something is not right in the world,' she will say, 'I don't see fried veg spring rolls in my dreams. The spiritual realm says there's no longer a normal cabbage soup being passed off as Chinese because it has soya. What happened to Chinese Bhel?' and she will promptly throw up all over herself and get down on her knees and say, 'Indians have stopped eating Chinese food made by Indians. They have really shown us. We will never have border disputes with India again.'

Of course, silliness also needs to be countered and multiple chefs in India had to come out and clarify that their chefs that made Chinese food were indeed Indian. Silliness is also occasionally indefensible.

Ramdas (and many others who shared his views) could have also mentioned what else Indians should boycott. This is a list of things that China created/invented that I have sourced from a historian friend of mine called Mr Vicky Pedia:

- GPS: The compass came from China
- Paper: Originated in China (this book)
- Printing: No more newspapers, books and especially those political hoardings (great)
- No more guns (good)
- Cookware and pottery: Even though I'm sure us Indians would have figured that out ourselves.
- Bricks: No more buildings should be allowed to collapse, which anyway frequently happens in Mumbai. Next time a building falls in India, please call that building a patriot.
- Oars: (Oars, really? We're giving their credit to China?

A long stick with paddles? Pretty sure multiple civilizations 'invented' these.)
- Acupuncture: Needles are only for medicines, vaccines and drug addicts.
- Cannons: This I'll miss. Every Tuesday, I make sure I fire my cannon at the annoying crows at my window.
- Chopsticks: (Kindly insert your own dandiya joke here.)
- Firecrackers: With pollution the way it is in India, this might be doubly patriotic.
- Flamethrowers: I love my flamethrower—especially if I want to barbeque something, impatiently—but country comes first.
- Gas cylinders: While China gets credit for inventing these, India figured out how to create a cycle of bribery and deceit around it—so, let's claim it.
- Helicopter rotor: Pretty hard for a helicopter to function without one and it raises the question of how helicopters flew before the rotor was invented. Either way, you can use that spare helicopter to entertain guests.
- Kite: This once again doesn't seem like an invention that India couldn't have figured out. I mean we have two festivals dedicated to this. But, again, country comes first.
- Oil refining and oil wells: I think we can figure out a way to do without oil. Except samosas are great (is that even the right oil?)
- Playing cards: (Sorry old people, talk to your relatives now.)
- Rockets: (Refer to guns)

- Soy sauce: (I'm sorry I need my soy sauce. We must draw a line somewhere, Mr Athawale—a line that is delicious, black and salty.)
- Tea: (Enough. Honestly, enough. This is too much. I can't take this anymore, Mr Athawale. India runs on important fluids and you can't just tell us to wake up naturally. Yes, there is coffee and I love coffee, but sometimes—every day—a man needs both.)
- Tofu: (Happy to boycott)
- Ice cream: (Mr Athawale, I'm sorry, but you're grievously misguided and let's sit together and have a Roasted Almond Ice Cream from Naturals or Praline from B&R and find a middle ground.)

Keep Ramdas Athawale's name in mind—it will come again.

There was also Ganesh Mandi who happens/happened to be the president of BJP's Asansol South Wing. Along with 15[58] other party workers, he burned an effigy to protest against China.[59] Burning effigies is fairly common in India and probably harks back to some Ravana complex or we just like controlled fire. I've never burned effigies, but I can understand the charm. You get some straw, some spare clothes and you make a nice doll and a printout of a face and then you burn it. What an incredible artistic expression. Taking something that you spent time on and burning it to ash, there's almost something Buddhist about it. I can sense the charm.

---

[58] https://www.youtube.com/watch?v=qnMSEtUzsOw. Accessed on 3 March 2022.

[59] 'Asansol BJP workers burn Kim Jong-un's effigy instead of Xi Jinping at China protest', *The Times of India*, 20 June 2020, https://timesofindia.indiatimes.com/city/kolkata/asansol-bjp-workers-burn-kim-effigy-at-china-protest/articleshow/76474556.cms. Accessed on 9 February 2022.

Additionally, if someone burns your effigy, consider yourself lucky that they're not burning you or attempting to injure or hit you, which is sometimes a pardonable offense in India if people disagree with you.

Either way, burning an effigy as a sign of protest is par for the course, except it was an effigy of Kim Jong-un who Mandi called, 'Prime Minister of China'. Let us presume that a man that can't tell apart the leader of North Korea from the leader of China will probably not research enough to find out that China's head of state is a president.

What is most absurd about this situation is the remaining 15 party workers—16 different humans could have had double-checked whether they were burning the right effigy or not. Sixteen opportunities to search on Google any of the following: President of China, PM of China, leader of China, king of China, whatever. But, alas.

When Mr Mandi was reprimanded for his mistake, he said, 'We were keen to register our protest and made a mistake in a hurry. I have already apologized to our district president, Lakshan Ghorui and assured him that such an error won't be repeated.'[60]

Though, it still remains to be seen if there is a district president with that particular name in Asansol and whether Mr Mandi was merely confusing a conversation he had with the captain of the local woman's volleyball team—anything is possible.

Due credit to Mr Mandi for at least accepting his mistake. There's a considerable number of politicians from parties in power who would commit considerably worse mistakes and

---

[60]Ibid.

then blame it on something that happened in 1949, as opposed to accepting any responsibility.

The government, of course, decided to take a stance against China and promptly decided to ban 59 Chinese apps in India, 58 of which no one really uses leaving behind TikTok that is used reluctantly by many.[61] The move was lauded by many as a stance taken by the Indian government and given the machinations of Indo-China diplomacy—it was *something*.

In India, TikTok was apparently under scrutiny for other issues—so, banning it was probably a relatively easy symbolic move. Of course, going by that logic, every single social media app is under some kind of scrutiny in India, so I withdraw my assessment. I have no issues with mainstream TikTok—it's not something I consciously consumed, but a lot of the content made a lot of people happy, so I was not too affected by its existence or lack thereof.

It did provide many Indians a platform to express themselves for probably the first time, giving them a voice— that was a good thing. And while most of it was complete nonsense, some of it was grassroots comedy of the highest standard and a lot of it was of the lowest standard.

I do know that I trended on TikTok for about five minutes in 2019 and it was stupidly easy, or so I thought since I never repeated the feat and amassed a sum total of 347 fans.

What I found absurd was people rejoicing about TikTok shutting down. Some were celebrating because apparently we had shown the Chinese something and others were celebrating

---

[61]'India bans 59 Chinese apps including TikTok, WeChat, Helo', *The Economic Times*, 29 July 2020, https://economictimes.indiatimes.com/tech/software/india-bans-59-chinese-apps-including-tiktok-helo-wechat/articleshow/76694814.cms?from=mdr. Accessed on 15 February 2022.

because they just hated everything about the app. Why? Because they didn't like the people on it, they didn't like what they created.

I vaguely understand that there were issues and accusations that TikTok faced, especially with regard to security and safety of minors (by vaguely understanding I mean I haven't done in-depth research of the topic)—that's severely important—but when you celebrate its defeat largely because you just didn't like it, you're in moral quicksand. Don't expect any empathy when something you like is banned. If the government bans PUBG or porn (already done—kind of?) or Bollywood, tambola nights, religious noise pollution (hmmm), casinos in Goa or whatever weird nonsense that keeps you sane—you're out of your depth asking anyone to stand with you.

I too have empathy for someone who loses a job, unless of course they're criminals. Whether you agree or disagree with TikTok, it supported over 2,000 employees, who were left without a job or an income for at least a few months.[62] Not a peep from anyone because screw TikTok, right? I don't like it and that's all that matters. #Blessed #UnBlessed

On the basis of certain reports, TikTok and its makers stand to lose about $6 billion from the India ban.[63] That's a surprisingly high number. That's $4.6 per Indian. I was not

---

[62] Dash, Sanchita. 'After firing hundreds of employees, Tiktok says it hopes to relaunch in India soon', *Business Insider*, 27 January 2021, https://www.businessinsider.in/tech/news/bytedance-lays-off-employees-in-india-months-after-tiktok-ban-in-the-country/articleshow/80476721.cms. Accessed on 4 March 2022.

[63] PTI, 'TikTok Expects Over $6 Billion Loss After India's Ban On App: Report', NDTV, 3 July 2020, https://www.ndtv.com/india-news/tiktok-expects-over-6-billion-loss-after-indias-ban-on-app-report-2256800. Accessed on 15 February 2022.

aware that the average Indian was spending ₹350 on TikTok, that's roughly the price of a ticket for a stand-up show. If I had known that lip-syncing to 'I'm a rider, a provider' or Paresh Rawal's dialogues from *Hera Pheri* would fetch me that much money, I would have switched my career way back in 2009. Never too late, though it definitely is too late now.

No one wants to see a balding father in his late 30s do that unless that person is David Warner, who frankly is more talented at that and everything else in life than me. Though, at the moment I may have a higher chance to make it to the Sunrisers Hyderabad than him.

Again, I will definitely judge you for enjoying a certain kind of content, but I will defend your right to enjoy whatever you want, if what you're creating is not grossly unlawful. I know many people feel that way about what I do as well, so…

The US—whether inspired by India or off their own volition—also threatened to ban TikTok and other Chinese apps. Of course, Donald Trump has a proclivity to make such threats and if all his threats were actually acted upon, he'd have invaded Venezuela, shut down a bunch of newspapers, arrested immigrants and possibly also built a wall to the moon.

Trump's statement was followed by China saying that they would ban American apps in China, which is a bit on the richer side, since China has already figured alternatives to every one of those apps using the simple technology of IP 'theft'.[64] Mark Zuckerberg started WeChat, Jack Dorsey started Sina Weibo, Jan Koum started Tencent QQ and there's also a Tinder-like app

---

[64]"China says US revoking of China apps ban a "positive step"', *The Economic Times*, 10 June 2021, https://economictimes.indiatimes.com/tech/technology/china-says-us-revoking-of-china-apps-ban-a-positive-step/articleshow/83401198.cms?from=mdr. Accessed on 15 February 2022.

called Momo, which just sounds wrong. And ironically, TikTok is not even called TikTok in China—it's Douyin.

China threatening to ban American apps in China is about as hollow a statement as many Indians who decided to boycott Chinese goods until Flipkart and Amazon started their August sales. Yes, that happened too.

It was not all half-assed and stupidity though.

China's business policies are often ruthless (like most big businesses?) and possibly illegal (fine line for most businesses?)—whether it's stealing IP or phone designs, cloning apps or significant security issues, etc., or just generally opportunistic practices that are probably unethical, but not really 'wrong', whether it's buying property across Australia, America, Asia (a strategy employed by Qatar and Middle East countries as well), or using the COVID-19 crisis to buy stock in companies that are briefly lowered.

It was like the Bank of China buying 1 per cent stake in HDFC, days after the pandemic and the lockdown.[65] It was akin to setting fire to your neighbour's lawn (allegedly), making sure he knew that you set fire to his lawn (allegedly) and then buying a cheap potted plant from him on OLX, because you know he needed the money. That plant was a money plant. Thank you, thank you, thank you so much—I am now retiring from comedy. I have peaked.

Foreign portfolio investments into NSE listed stocks from China rose to ₹3,257.67 crore at March-end 2020,

---

[65]Ramarathinam, Ashwin and Swaraj Singh Dhanjal. 'China's PBoC sells HDFC Stake', *Mint*, 10 July 2020, https://www.livemint.com/companies/news/china-s-central-bank-sells-hdfc-shares-11594385680034.html. Accessed on 9 February 2022.

from ₹774.12 crore in December 2019.[66] So, China decided that a pandemic that originated from their country was the right time to make some quick bucks. Why buy the cheaper money plant—get the car, buy the dog, sell the kids.

In April, this prompted the Indian government to ban automatic investments from China, mandating that all such investments get government approval first.[67] Of course, they didn't say China. India carefully said that this applies to any country whose border touches India. And since China has claimed the world as their border, this could literally apply to every country on Earth.

India also apparently told state and public sector companies to desist from issuing new contracts to Chinese companies[68]— fair enough, given the situation.

Of course, Indians quickly proved that we think purely on emotional basis and don't want to spend too much time on practical reasoning.

On one end, there is Sonam Wangchuk who said, 'You should stop using Chinese software in a week and hardware in a month,'[69] which is a reasonable expectation to make

---

[66]Ibid.

[67]Gupta, Shishir. 'India's hasn't changed its mind on Chinese investment, will make no exceptions: Officials', *Hindustan Times*, 23 February 2021, https://www.hindustantimes.com/trending/indias-hasn-t-changed-its-mind-on-chinese-investment-will-make-no-exceptions-101614092083010.html. Accessed on 15 February 2022.

[68]Inamdar, Nikhil. 'Can India afford to boycott Chinese products?' BBC News, 25 June 2020, https://www.bbc.com/news/world-asia-india-53150898. Accessed on 2 March 2022.

[69]'CHINA KO JAWAAB | Apke Sawalon ka Jawaab | Answers to Questions | Sonam Wangchuk | Ladakh', *YouTube*, https://www.youtube.com/watch?v=dfws1mZ56CY. Accessed on 2 March 2022.

and a well-thought out argument—if you want to do it, go ahead. Then there are other Indians who threatened to boycott Indian companies that had Chinese investments. They did so without even contemplating for half a second how many Indians would end up losing their jobs, how investments work, how much loss would that create for Indian companies and how much of the Indian economy has investments from China and others.

Of course things got political pretty quickly. The BJP accused Congress of getting donations from China for the Rajiv Gandhi Foundation (RGF) in 2005–06, up to the tune of ₹34 lakh, which honestly sounds like a pittance in political monies.[70] In political terms that's accusing your colleague of stealing one stapler pin.

Of course, the Rajiv Gandhi Foundation has not exactly been clear of controversies. In 1991, Dr Manmohan Singh had announced a sum of ₹100 crore to be allocated to RGF, which was obviously not entirely Dr Singh's idea.[71] The foundation is/was/will/could/might allegedly headed by 'someone else'—so, it's entirely possible that Dr Singh was merely a WhatsApp message to the parliamentary inbox.

The plan was revoked after criticism from the opposition and

---

[70] Tripathi, Rahul. 'Rajiv Gandhi Foundation had commissioned study "on export promotion to China"', *The Economic Times*, 10 July 2020, https://economictimes.indiatimes.com/news/politics-and-nation/rgf-had-commissioned-study-on-export-promotion-to-china/articleshow/76881543.cms?from=mdr. Accessed on 3 March 2022.

[71] IANS, 'Rajiv Gandhi Foundation got Rs 100 cr from Budget when Manmohan was FM', *Business Standard*, 26 June 2020, https://www.business-standard.com/article/current-affairs/rajiv-gandhi-foundation-got-rs-100-cr-from-budget-when-manmohan-was-fm-120062600478_1.html. Accessed on 9 Februay 2022.

then RGF, in a letter, said to the Parliament, 'The Foundation has thanked the government for its intention to donate a generous sum... However, the foundation has suggested that the best way to carry out this intention is for the government to identify suitable projects and programmes and fund them directly and implement them under its own supervision.'[72]

So sacrificial. The RGF was also accused of getting donations from banned Islamic preacher Zakir Naik. Congress netas countered this claim by first saying that they never received the money and then years later saying they returned the money[73], making it a weird puzzle. Can you return the money that you never received? Or did I just read all the news reports wrong? Did I read them or never receive them?

Zakir Naik claims the money was not returned.[74] Trusting a word of a man who endorses apostasy, subjugation of women, loathes every other religion, peddles hatred and once defended Osama Bin Laden saying, 'The thing is that if he's terrorizing the terrorist, he is following Islam.' 'Every Muslim should be a terrorist' is probably a bit of a stretch. A substantial stretch.[75]

---

[72]https://parliamentofindia.nic.in/ls/lsdeb/ls10/ses1/14020891.htm

[73]Jain, Bharti. 'Zakir Naik's NGO says it gave Rs 50 lakh to Rajiv Gandhi Foundation', *The Times of India*, 10 September 2016, https://timesofindia.indiatimes.com/zakir-naiks-ngo-says-it-gave-rs-50-lakh-to-rajiv-gandhi-foundation/articleshow/54258297.cms. Accessed on 9 February 2022.

[74]Banerjee, Anindya. 'Zakir Naik gave Rajiv Gandhi trust Rs 50 lakh. Congress says returned, Naik says no', *India Today*, 9 September 2016, https://www.indiatoday.in/india/story/sonia-rajiv-gandhi-foundation-zakir-naik-islamic-research-foundation-340231-2016-09-09. Accessed on 15 February 2022.

[75]Lakshmi, Rama. 'This Islamic preacher might have influenced one of the Dhaka terrorists. Now Indians want him banned', *The Washington Post*, 6 July 2016, https://www.washingtonpost.com/news/worldviews/wp/2016/07/06/did-an-indian-islamic-tv-evangelist-inspire-one-of-the-dhaka-terrorists-many-indians-say-the-preacher-must-be-banned/. Accessed on 15 February 2022.

In both cases—Zakir Naik and China—the Congress was accused of accepting donations to curry favours: one to look the other way while making hate speeches and one to endorse a free trade agreement. The accusations were pretty fierce and hit the political mark, except…

There is this wonderful thing called the PM CARES Fund. Started with the important purpose of raising funds to fight against COVID-19, the fund is surrounded by more lack of clarity than a trial Russian vaccine (I retract these words in early 2021 and would love a shot of Sputnik). At the moment of writing this, the documentation about its establishment is not publicly available, neither is its list of donors.

Some would say—and I am not 'some'—that it sounds a bit like an abstract version of the RGF. Some would say that I have not said it. I'm just echoing the thoughts of some who have told one, i.e., me. Some would also say that that sounds like an organizational version of an electoral bond. But, some are obviously mistaken.

It was also criticized for existing in the first place. Some (and in this case: many) said a fund called the Prime Minister's National Relief Fund (PMNRF) already exists to deal with such a calamity and with a considerably higher amount of transparency. The government, however, countered this by saying that the PMNRF does not allow for private donations and the disbursement of funds would be considerably slower than PM CARES.[76] Given the urgency of dealing with COVID-19, it's pretty hard to argue with this defence, except

---

[76]Jebaraj, Priscilla. 'How different is the PM CARES Fund from the PM's National Relief Fund?', *The Hindu*, 10 May 2020, https://www.thehindu.com/news/national/coronavirus-how-different-is-the-pm-cares-fund-from-the-pms-national-relief-fund/article31546287.ece. Accessed on 9 February 2022.

it is hard to defend why the list of donations and amounts are still not in public domain.

What was available in the public domain was that the PM Cares Fund got donations from individuals and corporate entities, including Xiaomi (₹10 crore), Huawei (₹7 crore), One Plus (₹1 crore) and the highest donation made was by a company called—hold your breath—TikTok, which gave ₹30 crore.[77]

The double irony of this is obviously not lost on anyone. TikTok donated to the PM CARES Fund and the PMO said they don't care about TikTok—see you later. That's the first irony. The second irony is that the government probably knew that after these donations had come in, accusations would follow soon. So, they decided that attack is the best form of defence and let's take up a donation from 15 years back, [name redacted]—go ahead, accuse the opposition before they can accuse us.

It's really smart.

It could be argued that the PM CARES Fund was for fighting the increasing number of deaths caused by the virus, and hence it was okay. To be perfectly honest, all rules went out the window in dealing with the virus. Then there was the third layer of irony: Chinese companies donated funds to an Indian PM to fight a virus that started in their country.

And then came the even more magical, fourth layer of irony to complete this cake of contradictions: some Chinese companies in India have a higher level of transparency with

---

[77]'Now banned TikTok gave Rs 30 crore to PM CARES Fund', *Business Today. in*, 30 June 2020, https://www.businesstoday.in/technology/news/story/pm-cares-fund-received-rs-30-crore-from-now-banned-tiktok-262711-2020-06-30. Accessed on 9 February 2022.

regard to their donations to India than certain organizations of our government(s).

It's relatively clear that political parties are innocent of all sins and crime when they're in power—out of power is another situation.

It's such a splendid tactic, it may have been—dare I say—very China-like politics in nature.

It's pretty hard to tell Indian people to boycott Chinese goods and funds when the political parties in power won't do the same. Additionally, unless things escalate dramatically at the border, it'll be significantly tough to boycott Chinese goods because of the way economics and global trade works. It's something the US discovered under Trump—and lessons learned by Trump are important lessons. I don't understand a lot of it, but it seems a personal decision for every individual Indian, and that's the purpose of a democracy.

Frankly, I definitely don't think they should return the money. The world and India has been floundering under the weight of this virus and so are people's finances. If you can afford to boycott Chinese goods and believe in the cause, then do it. If you can't, no one should shame you for not doing so. It's relatively easy to judge someone when you aren't aware of whether they have money to keep their family afloat.

Additionally, here's some facts about India and China:

Seventy per cent of India's drug intermediary needs are fulfilled by China[78]—I don't know exactly what this means, but next time a friend tries to offer me some narcotics, I

---

[78]Pandey, Kundan. 'COVID-19 exposes India's dependence on China for active pharma ingredients', *DownToEarth*, 7 April 2020, https://www.downtoearth.org.in/news/economy/covid-19-exposes-india-s-dependence-on-china-for-active-pharma-ingredients-70272. Accessed on 9 February 2022.

will call them an anti-national and tell them to buy locally sourced stuff, you traitor. (This is a joke—I don't even know what 'stuff' is, honestly.)

In the last five years, China has invested in 18 out of 30 Indian unicorns (start-ups worth $1 billion i.e., my monthly take-home).[79] There is a cumulative investment of $8 billion from China to India. Also, 3 per cent of our exports go to China.[80] This is not even taking into account manufacturers and traders in India that—like the rest of the world—rely on cheap Chinese labour and/or parts.

So while beating your chest about patriotism is all well and good, there are practicalities and economics involved that cannot really be squeezed into a WhatsApp forward about how India is the best. In 1962, Nehru made a colossal mistake of going to war with China. Today, we seem to constantly be sitting on the verge of an economic war, and unlike then, maybe we should be better prepared. Emotions and retweets and forwards don't necessarily contribute to GDP. If they did, India would be the richest country in the world. We'd be doing trade with other countries, selling 12,000 tonnes of outrage to Japan, 3,000 megatonnes of nationalistic pride to Norway and possibly at least 1 billion neutron stars worth of digital tears to the rest of the world.

We have to take a stance and Indians have done it, but be

---

[79] Bhattacharya, Ananya. 'China has invested a lot less in Indian startups than you think it did', *Scroll.in*, 19 November 2021, https://scroll.in/article/1010783/china-has-invested-a-lot-less-in-indian-startups-than-you-thought-it-did. Accessed on 4 March 2022.

[80] Bhowmick, Soumya. 'Chinese investments in Indian startups: Trends and controversies', Observer Research Foundation, 5 June 2021, https://www.orfonline.org/expert-speak/chinese-investments-in-indian-startups-trends-and-controversies/. Accessed on 9 February 2022.

smart. Here's an odd example: China faced a loss of ₹4,000 crore because of rakhi in India.[81] Because Indian traders and buyers decided to buy only made-in India rakhis. It shows you what's possible and also shows you how every Indian festival has a Chinese imprint. That's a true global power—when even the bond between an Indian brother and sister is renewed with a thread made in Shenzhen (probably).

Amongst others, Hero Cycles also decided to discontinue a deal of ₹900 crore with Chinese brands.[82] Fair enough for them, if they can afford to do that.

While this is happening globally towards China, let's not call it a boycott. It's more of a, 'Oh, sorry I didn't see you there. Sorry, lost your number. New phone (literally).' No country (US exempted) has come outright saying that they're boycotting China. Many businesses are moving from China to elsewhere and that should be good news for India, and it might be. About two dozen mobile manufacturing companies have pledged $1.5 billion to India and that number may rise up to $55 billion in five years, and contribute 0.5 per cent to India's economic output.[83]

---

[81]IANS, 'Imported Rakhi products from China to take Rs 4,000 cr hit: Traders' body', *Business Standard*, 22 July 2020, https://www.business-standard.com/article/economy-policy/imported-rakhi-products-from-china-to-take-rs-4-000-cr-hit-traders-body-120072201283_1.html. Accessed on 15 February 2022.

[82]ANI, 'Hero Cycles withdraws Rs 900 crore business plan from China', *The Times of India*, 8 July 2020, https://timesofindia.indiatimes.com/auto/news/hero-cycles-withdraws-rs-900-crore-business-plan-from-china/articleshow/76850094.cms. Accessed on 15 February 2022.

[83]Bloomberg, 'Over two dozen companies pledge $1.5 billion to set up mobile phone factories in India', *The Economic Times*, 18 August 2020, https://economictimes.indiatimes.com/industry/cons-products/electronics/over-two-dozen-companies-pledge-1-5-billion-to-set-up-mobile-phone-factories-in-india/articleshow/77582801.cms. Accessed on 9 February 2022.

And this is not only the result of COVID-19, but of the US–China trade war. India may stand to gain from that war, but we're many, many steps away from getting anywhere close to the infrastructure of manufacturing and trade in China.

Apple has started manufacturing in India, which means the Apple iPhone will at least save on shipping costs, using Vichare Couriers which is cheaper than Blue Dart in India (is it though, Sorabh?)

As for boycotting China, that remains a personal and a financial decision. Don't get bullied. If you can and want to, do it, if you can't afford to and don't want to, don't.

Support Indian goods and Indian comedians.

## What I'll Do When I Become PM

Once again as your future PM (Post Meridiem), I have a solution: a particularly wealthy (read: wealthy, not successful) businessman. This person has apparently suffered losses worth billions and that's why he's an inspiration to us.

Here's why: allegedly, his companies took substantial loans from banks that may or may not be associated directly or indirectly with China, and the gentleman and/or his companies were unable to settle those loans. Yes.

And here lies the key. Don't boycott Chinese products, take loans from Chinese banks, declare bankruptcy and don't pay the loans back. Take one for the team and India will celebrate you as a true patriot.

If all Indians do the same, we could buy out every Chinese bank and start our own HDFC in each of our homes and not allow China to buy 1 per cent of it.

(This idea is a satirical idea. Please don't default on loans.)

## *small thoughts*

*My wife was convinced she was suffering from insomnia. Seeing her night ritual of getting into bed at 11.00 p.m. and then scrolling through social media for hours every night, I'm pretty sure she's suffering from Internet, not insomnia.*

*That's a talented dad joke right there. Not insomnia, Internet. I have won dad-ness.*

*It seems most of us are suffering from the same affliction. We are obsessed with our phones and it's affecting our sleep patterns and the reason is simple—it's not that the Internet is free and fascinating and intoxicating and can help cater to whatever weird interests we have, it's because these god damn phones are too small.*

*As humans we should accept no responsibility for our actions and instead we should blame companies and other individuals. This is why I propose that all mobile phones should now be the size of a laptop and not so easy to use.*

*Like the European Union tells products to change themselves for privacy and security, I propose to be European Union 2.0 in India and propose this—ALL mobile phones should now be desktops.*

*All your browsing has to be done from the comfort of your desk and if you want to call someone you have to do it sitting up. I have ruined the mobile phone and app industry—but I've saved your sleep.*

*Please worship me via desktop.*

# 15

# *Pant Ki Baat: Episode One And Last*

## June 2021

*This was written at a point when vaccines were not easily available and well before India had given out over a billion vaccines—which is tremendously impressive, no matter how you look at it. At the time of writing this, getting a vaccination took days of sitting in front of your laptop for yourself and for others. Anyway, as I've mentioned a multitude of times in this book, things change.*

India's Prime Minister is known for not giving interviews or press conferences. He prefers monologues or conversations with students and officials that seem pre-approved (they may not be, but they sure seem that way). And his only interviews have been with journalists that LOVE him or actors that like him and mangoes. I'm not saying there's anything wrong with mangoes. In fact, few things reflect India more than mangoes: a delicious fruit that is available for only a few months in a year. Use that as a parable for whatever you want: bureaucracy, vaccine availability, whatever. I don't want to mess with the powerful Mango Lobby in this country—they may turn my heart into a hapoos, who knows?

He does, however, love to give monologues and speeches. Sometimes it seems like he wants to announce a new policy just so he can give a speech about it. That's one of the reasons why our Prime Minister is currently the Joe Rogan of India, having India's most popular audio format show.

Though, that's where the comparisons with Joe Rogan end, I think. I doubt Narendra Modi is into MMA, Fear Factor or other…um…things that Rogan is famous for. Narendra Modi's *Mann Ki Baat* (literally 'mind talk') has now run for seven years with monthly episodes directly from the mann of the PM. While the listenership of it cannot be tracked, the YouTube numbers of it tend to average about half a million. It also tends to average far more dislikes than likes, but let's not get ahead of ourselves.[84]

The show also raises questions about PM Modi's attitude towards interviews—where barring a couple that have involved softball questions about his diet or his work schedule (impressive whether you like him or not) or yoga—which have been few and none between.

Whether you disagree or agree: the PM is well within his rights to not do interviews. There is no law mandating him to give interviews; Rahul Gandhi did a couple and those pretty much sealed the fate of the Congress in the last general elections. So, why put yourself in the line of fire? When instead you can just talk about kids studying for exams? Why

---

[84]'Over 1 million 'dislikes' to PM Modi's Mann Ki Baat on BJP's YouTube Channel', *Mumbai Mirror*, 3 September 2020, https://mumbaimirror.indiatimes.com/news/india/over-2-5-lakh-dislikes-to-pm-modis-mann-ki-baat-on-bjps-youtube-channel/articleshow/77843783.cms. Accessed on 9 February 2022.

answer the bigger questions when you really don't have to? Why help a news channel sell ads for cement when you can talk about how cement is the pride of India?

Going forward, it seems to be the trend for the biggest politicians in India—doing interviews only with their biggest sycophants or a handful of foreign journalists, or doing their versions of Mann Ki Baat.

I'm not saying I should be PM, but Pant Ki Baat or even Mann Ki Pant seems a seamless transition. But, more on that later...

The theme of *Mann Ki Baat* is it is the happiest radio show out there. My friend comedian Atul Khatri does a show called *Only Positive News* and that may as well be *Mann Ki Baat*, which is in a way a strange output for a sitting PM. The show focuses on how our Olympians are preparing for the Olympics, our students are kicking ass, how we are making so many vaccines, how we are exporting so many vaccines, celebrating religious festivals, celebrating things in states that are ruled by your party, instead of vaccine shortage, petrol prices, unemployment, farmers' protests because those things are too much for the mann.

India must be positive under all circumstances. I guess since it's his show, he can do whatever he wants with it. Plus, the show has got four times more advertising on A.I.R.—so, that's probably going to help someone.

I don't have one of India's biggest podcasts—even though I've tried. Maybe when I join politics in 2038, I will have it, but I would like to take inspiration from PM Modi's show— say what you want about him, but the man is phenomenal at doing shows like this.

Here's a few things about his show that I noticed:

- As a YouTuber myself, it's quite well done. There's links for all the PM's social media accounts, his app and the MyGov app, as well as links to buy his book, which is just smart for post-PM plans. Get people following and get those followers, for now and forever. #InfluencerLife
- You have to watch/listen on 2X because he talks with tones that are more measured and thought out than some of his policies.
- YouTube Live chat, i.e., when the video released, is usually disabled. Though it was not always the case. It may be because over the last year, the show has got a ridiculous number of dislikes, the most being 1.2 million dislikes[85] for a video because it did not discuss the delay of the two major exams for engineering and medical students. The PM seemed unaffected by the hate—this is aspirational for YouTubers. Don't be dissuaded by hate and dislikes, just keep uploading videos, learn from one of India's top YouTubers, our PM. That's something Bhuvan Bam will not teach you. It's also indicative of how tough it may be to run a radio show as a sitting PM—no matter what you talk about, people are going to want you to talk about the thing you are not talking about.
- He talks to people who like his work and accepts

---

[85]'Over 1 million "dislikes" to PM Modi's Mann Ki Baat on BJP's YouTube Channel', *Mumbai Mirror*, 3 September 2020, https://mumbaimirror.indiatimes.com/news/india/over-2-5-lakh-dislikes-to-pm-modis-mann-ki-baat-on-bjps-youtube-channel/articleshow/77843783.cms. Accessed on 2 March 2022.

videos and audio clips from people who like what he does—that is again very smart. It's perfectly possible that the bad interactions are edited out, but still moving ahead with the happy YouTuber/radio show vibe. Good vibes.

- He also aims to keep *Mann Ki Baat* as an educational tool specifically for Indian students, so that there's a lot about general knowledge, good news and talk of exams. This is just smart because as a parent myself, if a YouTuber has gained interest with schoolkids, the parents will soon follow. And if you get consumers young, you will probably keep them for longer.
- He also frequently uses the term 'deshvaasiyon' i.e., country's inhabitants, as well as 'saathiyon', i.e., companions. He also used to use 'mitron', i.e., friends but, mitron became a meme, so now it's used sparingly. This is however a good endearing tool and I will attempt to use my own versions of the same.
- I may be wrong, but I don't think any rulers (sic) of other countries have a show like this: it honestly makes them appear like they missed a trick. Trudeau's *Canada Can!,* Imran Khan's *Loose Talk* (if you know, you know), Xi Jinping's *We Are All China!,* Jacinda Ardern's *A to NZ,* Biden's *Some Gibberish That Sound Like Words,* Putin's *Topless On Horse & Other Manly Tales, Me So Talkies with Mitsotakis* or *Merkel Germany Great Again* are wonderful pun opportunities, if not ideas for shows.

With all that in mind, I'd like to now do my version of *Mann Ki Baat.* Since this a book and not an audio version, please imagine that the words that you now read are a direct podcast for your brain. If it helps, you can hold this book close to your ear while reading it. I imagine my forthcoming speech will be broadcast sometime in 2032 or one year after you're reading this. This is based on the completely fictional scenario of me becoming PM which is about as likely to happen as Coldplay is to give a background score to a brand-new David Dhawan movie starring Govinda (it was all Yellow.)

Here it goes:

(PM Modi does his show in fantastic Hindi, but this will be in English, not because of some elitist convent school colonial hangover conspiracy, but because this book is in English because of some elitist convent school colonial hangover conspiracy.)

## *Pant Ki Baat*
Episode 1
Air date: Sometime in 2032/Never

'My dear country inhabitants. Much like you, I'm also a country inhabitant, friend. So, we are friends and country inhabitants, companions. And friends. There's a lot happening in the country, inhabitants. Unemployment is on the rise, petrol prices just touched ₹1 gold bullion per sniff, the WHO has said that the mandatory fourteenth dose of the vaccine for the last and most recent pandemic is now mandatory and the third dose for the new pandemic is also on its way, plus our neighbouring countries are waiting to stir up some stuff as always and the men's and women's cricket teams both just lost the World Cup Finals to Pakistan—things are not looking good.

So, let's ignore them and talk about something fun: exams and students.

Now, former PM Modi said in his book, *Exam Warriors,* that students should treat exams like a festival. I agree. But, I'd like to add that they should treat it like a festival where you make your fellow students look like idiots—a festival of condescension and domination. And it doesn't matter how much you get—you can still celebrate your marks and make your fellow classmates look like idiots.

I learned this from watching my daughter's sports day. Three kids won and were on the podium. The kid who finished no. 1 was crying his eyes out because the podium was too high, kid no. 2 was confused and the kid that finished at no. 3 was losing his mind celebrating because he was on the podium and not too far from the ground—so, he had no reason to fear.

And so, it doesn't matter where you land up—it just matters how much you enjoy it and make other people feel bad about finishing anywhere. In fact, the kids that didn't finish anywhere near the podium were also pretty happy with their tiny tetra packs of Frooti and Parle-G biscuits. So, the key to joy and not winning may be some form of sucrose.

Anyway, here's a guide based on whatever marks you score in your exams:

If you score 90+ per cent, oh look at you, you're a genius, unlike your fellow students who are dumber than bacteria.

If you score 80–90 per cent, oh, you're not a nerd like those scoring 90+, but an all-rounder. Studies aren't everything. You also play badminton/PUBG—those nerds probably know the history and the dates of badminton/PUBG, but have no clue how to play it. They probably think PUBG stands for

PhysicsUBiologyGeography. Hah, nerds.

If you score 70–89 per cent, there's no pressure on you. You are just a laidback person, quite relaxed. Above average, not below average. Towing the line, walking the fence, being cool. No pressure.

If you score 60–69 per cent, well, at least you got a first class. You couldn't get a first-class pass on the train, but there you go. You're exactly like the idiots that got 98 per cent. You got 61 per cent, but both of you are first class. So, who cares? Hah! You studied 0.5 per cent as hard as them and now look at you.

If you scored 35–59 per cent, well, you passed. Isn't that what life is about? Passing. After all, we all passed. And you're a back bencher. Yeah! Not like those nerds or those badminton players or those first-class pretenders. You're a back bencher, a rebel. You don't conform to society. Screw the patriarchy, the matriarchy, the hierarchy, the oligarchy. Wow, if you only knew such words you'd have scored more. But, who cares—ANARCHY!

If you scored below 35 per cent, all right! One more year of school. One more year of not having to worry about dealing with the world outside. Hah! While the rest of these idiots have to worry about college or secondary school, you can chill for one more year. Life is good. No pressure.

See, it's all about perspective. Personally, I got 70.83 per cent, barely sneaking into the second batch. And I don't know how to play PUBG, but I do know badminton. So, it's all good.

Anyway, unemployment is now up to 138 per cent and getting things back on track is tough, so, let's focus back on students, instead of talking about a job market that may or may not be there once you get to it.

People say marks don't matter and all these people are capitalists. (This is a pun that would make more sense if delivered in video because the statement itself makes no sense.) Marks definitely do matter. Those who say marks don't matter are people who didn't get the marks or people who have family backing. I qualify for both of the above, but I still know that they do. I've seen people around me score well in their boards or their entrance exams and change so much for their family and themselves.

For whatever it's worth, there's a lot of children in India that are the ticket to uplift their families to the next level. I've seen plenty of those kids and they're nothing short of incredible. One of those kids was my dad. I never saw him study for school in reality because my mother and him hadn't conceived of my existence till then and my DeLorean was being repaired—but I know he did.

So did my mom, but my dad will insist that his struggle was more real than hers. When both parents clear UPSC, they maintain competitiveness.

Anyway, I've seen and continue to see plenty of young Indians study their butts off, while working. One of my best friends growing up was a kid called Arvind. He used to press clothes with his dad in the morning, study through the day, play cricket with us, press clothes and then study some more. He's now a successful engineer working abroad—go tell him marks don't matter, while I ask him if I can crash at his place in Australia.

Marks matter, the pressure by the parents does not have to. If you're a parent and your kid seems like your ticket to more, that's fine, but let them also live a little. Yes, make them study, but give them some curiosity for the subject, motivate them, tell them why you think they're great and they can do this and also let them play cricket with their friends—because god damn it we need Arvind to bowl that off-cutter of his and get this a-hole from the other building out.

Anyway, reports have just come in that there is a fresh border dispute with China who now claims Delhi as part of PRC—so, let's talk about fitness.

Country inhabitants, fitness is the key to a good life. It creates all these good chemicals in your mind and also helps you enjoy alcohol way more. Have you ever had a pint of beer after a two-hour walk? What could be more delicious? It's what Usain Bolt and other fitness experts ignore about fitness—it makes you really enjoy your alcohol.

According to fitness experts around me—my wife—fitness holds the key to your moods. This is especially applicable to me. If I am unhappy for four days and snapping at everyone, I realize a simple thing: I need to lift some weights. And the change is almost immediate.

Before working out I think to myself, 'Life—what is it? Why does it exist? What is my place in the world? Do I have a place in the world? I am placeless, useless, friendless and incapable of achieving anything.'

Minutes after working out I think to myself, 'That Dwayne "The Rock" Johnson—I'm pretty sure I could kick his ass.'

Exercise is essentially healthy alcohol. Think about it: it makes you feel stronger, looser, happier and more relaxed. Plus, it has the upside of not making you feel like shit the next day. Unless it was leg day—then congrats on moving your feet.

I do recommend exercise to our students much like PM Modi did. Whether it's yoga, weight training, calisthenics or running up the stairs carrying your school bag, do it all. I can't guarantee it will get you more marks, but I can guarantee it'll make you feel a little better about whatever you scored.

Anyway, I also hear there's an explosion at an oil refinery where 16 people had their heads deep fried—so, let's talk about one more tip for students. If you're a bad student, always have the insurance of having a more intelligent sibling. I had that insurance in the shape of an elder sister who ensured that she was a top-five student in her school so, I could be the middle-five student in my school. The pressure was off me, the expectation was on her and so her getting 90 per cent was equal to me barely passing—it was perfect.

If you don't have such a sibling, start looking. It's too late to tell your parents to create a sibling for you so you're going to have to improvise and help them adopt. Ideally someone older than you. Here's what I suggest you do—find the toppers in your school, ideally one who does not have any parents and you tell your parents to adopt that orph...'

This is when the video will be abruptly stopped. Probably by R&AW or the CBI or the BCCI or one of those important organizations in India. And thus will end my attempt to address the people of India and especially its students.

I did not even get the chance to cover the news updates such as:

'...the BCCI did eventually buy out Air India, Vijay Mallya got a brand new haircut, all news channels are now advertisements, being a motivational speaker is the no. 1 job in the country, bribery is now legal and non-bribing is a criminal offense, 3,000 criminals from abroad have bought Diamond visas to live in India bringing $8 billion to the exchequer, rumours on WhatsApps are now gospel, old-school nepotism in Bollywood has been replaced by nepotism in

Bollywood by outsiders that made it and finally I'd like to thank Richvender Singh, Fatima Dollar, Ameer Tripathi, Gulabuddin Chequewalla, Richa Rich, all the names in the Panama Papers and of course, Sorabh Pant, i.e., myself for paying income tax.' I could not even close with my message of, 'Don't forget to subscribe, like and share MyGov and bulk buy my new book, *Marks Do Matter, But You Don't*. Good bye, country inhabitants.'

Well, I just did. And this is yet another reason I will never and should never be your PM. Vote for someone better than me. Or better than whoever is running.

## small thoughts

*It occurs to me that most of our politicians seem to come from echo chambers and homogeneous backgrounds that only tend to amplify their own opinions and their own specific culture.*

*Maybe it should be a mandatory seven-day workshop to make it to the state or national legislature that you have to spend time in a dormitory with people from all the different religions, castes and economic background as you.*

*And it should be mandatory that you spend at least two hours talking to at least 20 of them. Maybe it will still keep these politicians as focused on their agendas as before, but maybe it will remind them that the world exists outside their own specific behinds.*

*This would be a great idea for comedians, writers, journalists, directors because a lot of us (including myself) have made similar errors in our careers of talking nonsense about people and topics we don't understand.*

*I just realized I'm describing school. Or at least how schools should be.*

# *And Another Thing...*

In 2021, around June—I remember the month very specifically for some reason—I had been feeling absolutely defeated. This had gone on for two months—just a feeling of melancholy and immense hopelessness. There were plenty of dark images I had been dealing with in my head. The circumstances of the world around us—the deaths, the anger towards the death and everything it entailed, fear for those around me, fear of those around me, a horrible couple of months of earning and a significant amount of online trolling and hate, some personal things that I'll get into at a later date or maybe never, all of them—had formed a khichdi of anxiety and sadness.

Plus, this was after months of all kinds of people calling me out for all kinds of jokes from the past. Some of them I felt deeply apologetic and sorry for (which I acknowledged repeatedly on YouTube Lives)—some of them just pointedly unfair.

I didn't feel like I could move. My brain was sinking, it felt as if my head was pushing me down, the chemicals in my mind weighing a ton and dragging me down. The weight on my own shoulders and my own mind became too much to bear, for months.

To be honest: a variation of that feeling has been a tourist in my mind quite often. Dropping in and out once a year and I've always been able to fight it off. But, this persisted. I questioned every little word that I ever said and every word that I would ever say and wondered if I was wrong to say and if someone would misconstrue it.

Maybe it was a sense of guilt for having said stupid shit in the past or maybe it was just a gnawing fear that something was wrong with everything I thought of the world. I began to wonder if I was all the things people called me or if the world had just gone mad and some of us had to be crushed under it.

I began to fear where I would get the next bit of work from and if my front door would rattle delivering a note for the end of my career. Maybe that's why so many people used to write in to me and tell me exactly why they hated me. Maybe, I deserved all of it. Guilt, fear, anxiety, paranoia all at once. What a wonderful time.

It seems like an exaggeration now, but that's what was going on in my head. The truth is that during the pandemic and being caged in your own house and being caged inside your own mind, we've all faced a variant of the same. So, my deepest sympathies if you've felt the same. I send you mental hugs from across the atmosphere.

It took some effort to pull myself out and I'm still in the process of doing the same, but I fear it will return. I fear the demons in my head and the people that don't recognize what they're doing to people with words that they say online—of which I was one. And still may be in the future.

I've said so much rude stuff to people in my career as a comedian—some of it was deserved and some of it just utterly undeserved. Maybe that was coming right back to me.

Every single person who has ever called out another person for something that's led to an avalanche of other people also piling on to the person will not understand what it feels to be the subject of their derision or hate. It's only when the avalanche descends upon you that you may conceive your own screams that caused the snow to pile on in the first place.

I hope that never happens to you, but given that hateful trolls as well as 'moral' warriors and people that just enjoy virtue signaling are not too far removed from each other, it probably will. Some of them are righteous, but even they are drowned by the above.

We're all fallible, we all make mistakes and we're all people. And most of us are also capable and driven to evolve our thinking and our mind. So, if you're part of a mob (whether you think you're right doesn't matter), at least attempt to be a nice mob. You're attacking real people, not social media handles.

Additionally, if I've ever said something (or say something) to you in the past which has made you feel bad, inferior, humiliated or worse: that was never my intention. And my deepest apologies for the same.

I say this not out of fear of further retribution, but genuine sadness that something I said would make someone feel the way I've also felt at the worst points in my own life. A lot of us make similar journeys, but in different vessels.

The truth is: I don't know what may trigger people in the future and what the rules of engagement will be in the long run, but most of us are learning. So, give each other that little modicum of patience to do so.

Literally, all I want to do is make people laugh. Because the only thing that's kept me sane from the time I was a kid is laughter. If in the pursuit of that I've said something that affected you, then I apologize. Hopefully we can laugh together again. And we can feel light about the world and laugh at the things around us without repercussions, which honestly is a really tough balance to achieve.

Hopefully, this book has had moments that made you feel that way. Hopefully, I helped you forget.

Hopefully, we can do this again sometime.

Hopefully, some of these bits will be out as stand-up and I get to cheer you up (for a small price) twice.

Hopefully, we can converse, disagree, learn and then have a laugh.

Hopefully.

Take care of yourself and those around you.

# *Acknowledgments*

There's one person without whom I would never have been able to write or finish this book—so, I would love to thank myself. Sorabh, thanks a lot for keeping at it despite several moments of confusion, being overburdened, overwhelmed and underwhelmed by your own writing. And especially writing the 10 chapters that you had to remove because of fear and anxiety caused by self-doubt and the world we live in.

I'd also love to thank my publishers at Rupa—Kapish Mehra, for greenlighting this book and also giving me an advance cheque at a time during the pandemic where my bank account had more emptiness than my soul; Saswati Bora, my editor and occasional bouncing board, who has had considerable patience for all the delays caused by circumstances. Though she got to go for long walks (legally), I feel life has rewarded her well for editing this book.

My sister, Meghna Pant, has been significantly involved in the editing of all my previous books and this is the first one she's not been involved in at all. But, I'm putting her in here because otherwise she'll once again tell the world that I'm ungrateful and a terrible person who refuses to credit her for anything. Here's your credit, Meghna.

Also, do check out Meghna's many books that exist out there—*One & a Half Wife*, *The Terrible, Horrible, Very Bad Good News* and *How to Get Published in India*. Now you give me credit.

This pandemic was a bizarre time for my wife, Iva Bagchi, and me. It started off rocky because our minds were getting adjusted to the new world and then over months we've gotten closer, calmer and happier than we've ever been in our married life. And it mainly has to do with my wife doing a tonne of yoga, learning how to teach yoga and being calmer and happier with herself, our kids and me. She also likes the darkest and weirdest jokes that I write—which no one except her seems to approve of.

So, I would like to thank yoga. And hopefully, I will also find the same calmness one day.

I'd also like to thank you. Whether you bought this book because you enjoyed my other works or were curious or because the book is on severe discount because of lack of sales or because you thoroughly dislike my work and wanted to find another reason to dislike me—that's all good. I'm happy to talk to you either way and I hope we can move forward in this social media world with some understanding and humanity as opposed to hatefulness and accusations.

Quite randomly I'd also like to thank a lot of my YouTube members who have sustained me with their love, support, opinions and breaking news on WhatsApp. I was surprised at our sudden friendship and it has meant a lot to me as have your Super Chats, gifts and kindness. Special mention to Rajat Shah, Kajol Agarwal, Sharanya Deva, Kaustubh Bhalerao—you all know why. And Diptish, Ishwari, Akhil, Hiren, Pratima, Anmol—you all also know why.

I'd also like to thank my parents, Sujata Pant and Deep Pant. The things they've done for me throughout my life and significantly during the pandemic make me ridiculously emotional and tear up. Drinking and arguing politics or agreeing on cricket with them is one of my favourite things to do and I hope we can do that for many years to come.

Also, please lend me some money—this book didn't pay as much as you think it did.

If you enjoyed my words, do:

- Send out a Tweet (@hankypanty),
- Tag on Instagram (@sorabhpant),
- Super Chat on my YouTube Live channel (Youtube.com/1phuntru)
- Give a like on all my stand-ups (YouTube.com/PantOnFire), where I release a clip from stage twice a month (at the time of writing). I'm also on LinkedIn and Facebook for some reason. And will eventually get on OnlyFans.

Made in the USA
Monee, IL
03 May 2026